ALLAN PINKERTON,

AMERICA'S FIRST PRIVATE EYE

Books by Sigmund A. Lavine

ALLAN PINKERTON

America's First Private Eye

BY SIGMUND A. LAVINE

ILLUSTRATED

DODD, MEAD & COMPANY

NEW YORK

For Dorothy:
who had faith in both Pinkerton and the author

ACKNOWLEDGMENTS

The clues that enabled me to "shadow" Allan Pinkerton in order to report his career as a sleuth in peace and a spy for his country in war and to tell the story of the world's oldest and largest private detective agency came from many sources. One of the best was Allan Pinkerton himself, who graphically recorded many of his adventures in eighteen fascinating volumes. Nearly as helpful were the writings of Richard Rowan, historian of the art of espionage and chronicler of crime. Other authors also furnished clues which led to files of musty newspapers and bound volumes of long-forgotten magazines. I am grateful to them all.

However, I particularly want to thank for "information received" George F. O'Neil of Pinkerton's National Detective Agency who, more than anyone else, has made this book possible. Special thanks are also due to: Ivan Sandrof, literary editor of the Worcester *Telegram-Gazette;* Jane Manthorne, reading advisor to young adults at the Boston Public Library; the entire staff of the Milton Public Library; and, finally, my good friends in the reference room of the Boston *Herald* who have, as always, found what I wanted in the "clips."

—SIGMUND A. LAVINE

Illustrations

The following illustrations with the exception of the final one are reproduced through the courtesy of the Pinkerton's National Detective Agency, Inc.

President Lincoln holds a conference at the battlefront with General McClellan and Allan Pinkerton ("Major Allen")

ALLAN PINKERTON,

AMERICA'S FIRST PRIVATE EYE

WE NEVER SLEEP

"The thoughts of youth are long, long thoughts . . ."
—Longfellow

Tʜɪs ɪs ᴛʜᴇ sᴛᴏʀʏ of Allan Pinkerton who came to the United States to avoid arrest, became an internationally famous private detective and founded the world's oldest and largest investigative agency. While his capture of jewel thieves, bank robbers and swindlers filled the newspapers of his day, Pinkerton also has a place in the history of his adopted country. A man of great powers of observation and courage, he prevented an assassination attempt on Abraham Lincoln; organized the first official Secret Service for duty behind Confederate lines during the War Between the States; and rode with lawmen along the Old Frontier, hunting down members of Jesse James's gang, the Reno brothers and other desperadoes who bragged about the number of notches on their guns. Called upon to fight crime by local, state and federal authorities, Pinkerton trained his two sons, William and Robert, to assist him and, in time, they became almost

1

as famous as their father. Although much of the criminal investigation that brought "The Pinks" fame has been taken over by the F.B.I. and other modern police organizations, Pinkerton's National Detective Agency still tracks down lawbreakers in the colorful tradition of its founder—America's first private detective.

* * *

"Lower away!"

Allan Pinkerton watched anxiously as the lifeboat containing his wife dropped jerkily toward the water. In spite of the bellowed commands of the second officer, he did not leave the rail until he saw the craft pull away from the side of the ship. Then he hurriedly took his assigned position in another boat.

"Grab aholt, mate," grunted a burly sailor as he unshipped an oar. "The harder we row, the sooner we'll be on shore."

It couldn't be any too soon for Allan. He had to find Joan and comfort her. What a honeymoon voyage this had been! Ever since leaving Scotland, their vessel had been constantly buffeted by gale winds and high seas during one of the worst storms of the year 1842, and the Pinkertons had been unable to go out on deck—and now they were shipwrecked! Yet worried as he was, Allan chuckled when he recalled that his wife had solemnly assured the captain, two days ago, that they would have smooth sailing for the rest of the trip.

Joan, Allan decided as he rowed, might be the bonniest lass that ever came from Edinburgh, but she certainly couldn't forecast the weather. For the past forty-eight hours, the wind had blown with hurricane force and their ship, driven over two hundred miles off course, instead of making its landfall, Halifax harbor, had piled up on the sand bar off Sable Island, near the coast of Nova Scotia, known to seamen as the "Graveyard of the Atlantic."

While the Pinkertons were honeymooners—Allan and Joan had been married the night before they sailed—the voyage to Canada was not a pleasure cruise. If Allan had remained in Scotland, he would have been arrested as an enemy of the Crown, since he was considered a dangerous agitator because of his activities in the Chartist movement. This was a revolt of the workingmen of the British Isles against the political power of the wealthy landlords. Although most Chartists were content to petition Parliament and march in monster demonstrations, Pinkerton belonged to a group that believed that they would gain recognition sooner by staging riots.

Yet, strangely enough, Allan's father, William Pinkerton, a Glasgow police sergeant, had died as the result of injuries received while trying to maintain order during a Chartist riot. Allan Pinkerton, who had been born on August 25, 1819, was barely ten when left fatherless and he and his brother Robert were forced to go to work. His first job was running errands for a patternmaker. Although there was plenty to see in Glasgow, Scotland's largest city, as Allan carried parcels to dockyards and factories on both sides of the Clyde River, the boy was not happy. He wanted to learn a trade.

Two years later, he got his wish. William McCauley, a cooper, indentured him as an apprentice. For seven years Allan learned to make barrels and casks and became a master craftsman. While working for Mr. McCauley, despite what had happened to his father, Pinkerton became a Chartist. He was sincerely convinced that the demands of the "People's Charter" for political reform were just.

Between working in the shop by day and plotting with other hotheads at night, Allan had been too busy to set a

wedding date with his fiancée, Joan Carfrae. Then, a secretly whispered warning by a former associate of his father changed everything. Within a few hours he was both
a married man and a wanted criminal fleeing to the New
World, to start life anew among other English-speaking
people in Canada. Pinkerton realized that he had been
extremely lucky. Yet, grateful as he was now, if only he
knew Joan was safe, he would gladly exchange his seat
in the lifeboat for a prison cell.

Joan was safe, but like many of the other passengers
who had reached shore, the eighteen-year-old bride was
trembling with fear, for, no sooner had their boats
grounded than a band of Indians dashed out of the woods
and surrounded the party, demanding that the women
hand over their jewelry. As most of the passengers were
poor immigrants, there were very few trinkets that attracted the Indians, but they all wanted Mrs. Pinkerton's
wedding ring.

In the *Chicago Daily News* for May 27, 1931, Joan
Pinkerton Chalmers, the great detective's daughter, reported:

> Father, in later years, told us how mother resolved to
> cling to her wedding ring, in spite of all the danger, and how
> he, feeling sure that the Indians would take it forcibly, said
> to her, "Oh, give it to them, Joan, and I will get you another
> ring." She then surrendered it. But—though in later years she
> wore many rings—she would never wear another wedding
> ring. No other ring to take the place of that precious symbol
> of her marriage.

After robbing the passengers, the Indians disappeared.
The next day, members of the crew managed to salvage
a few of the Pinkertons' meager possessions from the ship,
and the couple boarded a passing schooner bound for

the mouth of the St. Lawrence River. As they walked the deck, Allan turned to Joan and said, "Lass, we're going to the United States! My mind's made up. And I know just how we'll get there. I asked the captain and he told me that the easiest way is for us to take a boat through the Great Lakes to Detroit."

The chances are if Joan had asked her husband why he had changed his mind about settling in Canada, he could not have given her a single reason. Nor could Pinkerton explain later why, after reaching Detroit, he bought an old spavined horse, a patched set of harness and a ramshackle wagon—it just seemed the right thing to do. After stowing away some simple camping necessities, such as blankets and cooking pots, plus the few odds and ends of clothing saved from the wreck, and lifting Joan up on the seat, Allan took his place beside her, slapped the reins and shouted, "Get up there—we're on our way to Chicago!"

It was a long, weary trip, over rutted and dusty roads. In order to pass the time, Allan and Joan asked each other riddles, told stories and sang as the wagon rolled along. Late each afternoon, they began looking for a camping spot where they could find drinking water, wood for a fire and a place for the horse to graze. After cooking supper and washing the pots and dishes, the tired couple would roll up in blankets and were soon fast asleep. When it rained, the Pinkertons were forced to take shelter in the hayloft of some friendly farmer's barn. They could not afford to pay for a night's lodging in an inn. Their entire fortune consisted of a silver dollar wrapped up in a handkerchief.

Finally, the couple reached Chicago. Allan hailed a passer-by and asked where he could find a respectable, clean, inexpensive boarding house. Following directions,

he pulled up to the door of the place suggested and soon
came to terms with the owner. When the wagon was un-
packed and Joan made comfortable, he drove to the nearest stable. After several hours of dickering, he returned
to his wife with money in his pockets for the first time
in weeks—the proceeds from the sale of the horse, harness
and wagon. It was not a large amount, but Allan was
sure that long before it was all spent for food and lodging,
he would have a job.

However, jobs were scarce in Chicago. Although five
years had passed since the Panic of 1837, the city was
still feeling the pinch of "hard times." Allan walked from
cooperage to cooperage, seeking work. No matter where
he went, all he heard was, "Sorry, we don't need any
help."

Weary, worried and greatly discouraged, Pinkerton, as
a last resort, introduced himself to some fellow Scots
who were well established in Chicago, and asked if they
could help him. Thanks to their efforts, Allan was hired
to make barrels at Lill's Brewery. For working from early
morning until six at night, he received fifty cents a day.

On Sundays, unable to afford to pay for other forms
of recreation, the Pinkertons would take long walks along
the curving shore of Lake Michigan. As they strolled,
Allan would talk of the day when he would own his own
shop. His wife encouraged this ambition and was delighted when, after working at Lill's for a year, Allan announced, "Well, lass, you've always said that when I
found the right place to set up for myself, you'd gladly
leave Chicago. The time has come for you to pack. They
need a cooper in Dundee."

"Allan, don't tell me we're going back to Scotland!"

"Of course not—Dundee's a town of about three hundred people, on the banks of the Fox River, thirty-eight

miles northwest of here. It was settled by Scots, that's the reason for its name. There's a post office, a blacksmith shop, a couple of inns and several stores. The place is the trading center for a large farming area, but there's no cooperage, so it's the ideal place for us, because farmers need barrels."

Two weeks later, the Pinkertons were settled in a long, one-story wooden house surrounded by a garden. It was located on a hill just three hundred yards from the planked oak bridge that spanned the Fox River and combined a shop with living quarters. Joan happily went about her housekeeping duties in the front of the building, while Allan worked long hours in the rear, proudly advertising himself as the "Only and Original Cooper of Dundee."

2

"A policeman's lot is not a happy one!"
—Gilbert

ALMOST FROM THE DAY that Allan hung up his sign, he
did a flourishing business. Farmers quickly discovered that his barrels and casks were stoutly made, priced
fairly and always ready for delivery when promised. However, Pinkerton took in very little cash. The barrels were
swapped for produce which Allan sent to Chicago to be
sold or bartered for goods which he could use or trade. As
his reputation grew, he found it necessary to hire a helper
to fill his orders. Before long, he employed a crew of eight
men in the shop. Most of them were German immigrants
who sang and whistled as they worked, beating time with
adz or mallet.

Thrifty by nature, Allan saw no reason to buy poles
to make barrel hoops when they could be had for nothing.
So one day he left the shop in charge of his foreman and
rowed out to an island in the middle of the river to cut a
supply. It was commonly supposed in Dundee that the is-

land was uninhabited, but Pinkerton, a most observant individual, noticed that the grass and bushes were bent back, making a path from the shore. Curious, he followed it and in a thick stand of trees found a campsite that appeared to be used quite frequently.

Pinkerton decided to tell Sheriff Yates of his discovery. However, that would have to wait. Unsheathing his ax, he set to work chopping down saplings which he loaded in his skiff, taking them back to the mainland. After storing the poles in his shop, Allan went to see Yates, described what he had seen and suggested, "Perhaps some of the horse thieves or counterfeiters that you've been looking for are using the island as a hide-out, Sheriff."

"You could be right, Pinkerton; you could be right! I'd take it kindly if you'll go over there with me and show me what you found."

After visiting the island, Yates agreed that there was something suspicious about the campsite and asked Allan to help him watch it. One of the coopers rowed the two out every evening and picked them up in the morning. During the night, Pinkerton and the sheriff took turns standing guard. A week passed, but the only sound they heard on the island, with the exception of their own voices, was the hoot of an owl. Then, one rainy night, when both men, cold and wet, were thinking longingly of their comfortable beds and wishing the other would suggest calling the watch off, they saw a light gleaming through the underbrush. From behind a fallen log, the pair peered out cautiously. They saw a gang of men carrying heavy sacks. "Get your gun out, Pinkerton," whispered Yates. "I'm going to find out what they've got in those sacks."

They proved to be filled with counterfeit coins. While

the sheriff held the gang prisoners at gunpoint, Allan went to the riverbank and fired three shots in rapid succession— a prearranged signal—and soon a half dozen skiffs, manned by sturdy coopers, arrived to assist in taking the counterfeiters to jail.

Awakened by the shots, the entire population of Dundee was waiting on the shore when the posse landed. After locking up the gang, Yates told the shivering crowd how Allan's discovery of the campsite had made their arrest possible. Pinkerton was embarrassed and, as soon as he could get away from his back-slapping neighbors, he went home to bed. However, the villagers considered him a hero and delighted in telling strangers about the smart detective work on what they now called Bogus Island— so named because of the counterfeit coins captured there.

Yates, impressed by Pinkerton's powers of observation, became a frequent caller at the shop, constantly asking Allan's advice about the cases he was investigating. Although Allan had to stop work to chat with the sheriff, he did not mind. In fact, Joan accused him of being more interested in crime that cooperage. Nevertheless, he probably never would have become a famous detective if two Dundee businessmen had not sent for him on a July day in 1847.

When their messenger arrived, Pinkerton, bareheaded, barefooted, dressed in overalls and a hickory shirt, was splitting staves. Without stopping to put on his shoes, he hurried to Hunt's General Store, where he was greeted by the owner and one of his friendly competitors, Increase Bosworth.

The latter said, "Allan, Henry and I have a job for you in the detection line."

"Now, look here—just because I helped Yates—"

"Helped nothing, you did all the work when it came to

spotting the hide-out. Listen to me. We're sure that there still is a counterfeiter operating in Dundee. Oh, we've no evidence, but a stranger has been asking where he can find old man Crane—and, while nobody's been able to prove it, all the storekeepers along the river suspect that Crane's the distributor of counterfeit money in these parts."

"Then too, Allan," interjected Hunt, "every time a shady character comes to Dundee, he always asks the way to Libertyville and Crane's house. So when a respectable-looking, but smooth individual rides up and asks where Crane lives, it seems more than likely he's the one who supplies the old man with worthless bills drawn on George Smith's bank."

Although Pinkerton had no bank account, he knew all about Smith. A Scotsman from Aberdeen, Smith had organized the Wisconsin Marine and Fire Insurance Company whose charter gave it the right to engage in banking. Because the bank notes issued by the firm—called "George Smith's money"—were always redeemable in specie at full face value, merchants throughout the Northwest accepted them, while the notes of most local banks were either discounted or refused by businessmen. While Allan knew that Smith's money was considered "good as wheat" by farmers and bankers, he realized that he could not tell a real ten-dollar bill from a counterfeit one, so he said frankly, "I don't figure how I could help you. What do I know about counterfeiting? Moreover, I never saw a ten-dollar bill in my life!"

"Oh, come on, Allan!" exclaimed Hunt. "You're wasting time. That stranger is down at Walker's harness shop, getting his saddle fixed."

"What can I do?"

"Do? Why, the best you can, of course!"

So, with no plan of action, Pinkerton wandered slowly down the street to the harness shop. Tied to the hitching-rack was a sleek roan horse, but Allan, more interested in the animal's owner, went inside the building and immediately picked out the stranger in the usual crowd of loafers that hung about Walker's.

Years later, recalling his first assignment as a detective, Pinkerton described the man as follows—"nearly six feet in height, weighed fully two hundred pounds, was at least sixty-five years of age, and was very erect and commanding in his appearance. I noticed all this at a careless glance, and also that his hair was dark, though slightly tinged with gray, and his features very prominent. His nose was very large, his mouth unusually so, and he had a pair of the keenest, coldest small gray eyes I have ever seen, while he wore a large, plain gold ring on one of the fingers of his left hand."

All this Pinkerton saw "at a careless glance"! No wonder that, as the years passed, criminals all over the world were to fear his wonderful powers of observation and marvelous memory.

Seeing that Walker had nearly completed the repairs for the stranger, Allan drifted outside and was patting the roan horse when the man left the shop with his saddle. As any countryman would do, Pinkerton helped him adjust it, and, while they tightened straps and buckles, the suspect asked in a low voice, "Friend, can you tell me where old man Crane lives?"

"Go over the river and swing east," Pinkerton answered out of the corner of his mouth. "When you get to the Miller place, ask again. 'Course if you don't want folks to know where you're going, turn northeast at the fork and, when you get to Libertyville, you'll have no trouble finding Crane."

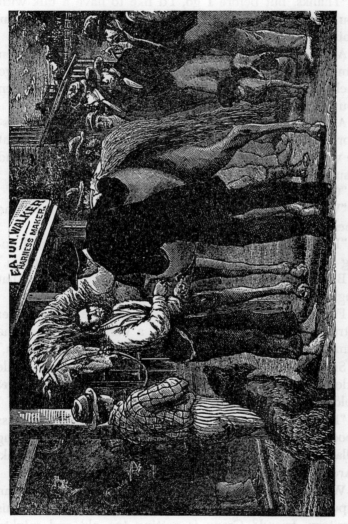

Pinkerton recognizes a counterfeiter.

"Thanks, but before I go, I'd like to have a talk with you. I'm sure that what I have to say will be worth your while. How about meeting me across the river?"

Allan agreed, realizing that the stranger had mistaken him for one of Crane's associates. "Just give me time to go back home and put on my boots," he said, "then, when you see me cross the bridge, come along."

As Pinkerton was pulling on his boots, Hunt and Bosworth came to the cooperage and Allan told them what he was going to do. The storekeepers were delighted and assured him that he could capture the stranger.

"Capture him? How?"

"Why, get some of his bills and then hold him for the Sheriff."

"I'm not worried about holding him, but how am I going to get any bills? I haven't any money to buy them."

Bosworth handed him fifty dollars and said, "That ought to be enough. Good luck, Allan."

Fifteen minutes later, in a wooded ravine, the stranger introduced himself as John Craig, a Vermont farmer, who came west every year to conduct some "special business."

Sure of his man, Pinkerton admitted, "Once in a while I do some special business too—that is, providing I can get hold of first-class goods."

"I figured you were a smart one and if it is first-class goods you want, take a look at these," said Craig, offering Allan two counterfeit notes on George Smith's bank. "Aren't they beauties?"

While Pinkerton examined the notes as if he were an expert, Craig continued, "Why don't you take over this territory, friend? Crane is getting too old and mighty careless, from what I hear. You could make a pile."

"How much would I have to buy?"

"Between five hundred and a thousand at twenty-five cents on the dollar—cash."

"I haven't got that much money with me. Here's what I'll do. I'll take five hundred if you meet me at the unfinished church at Elgin at four this afternoon."

After shaking hands, the two separated. Craig jogged on toward Elgin, while Pinkerton hastened back to Dundee where he reported to Hunt and Bosworth the arrangements he had made with Craig. They gave him one hundred and twenty-five dollars to buy the counterfeit bills. At the cooperage, Allan ate lunch, talked briefly to his foreman and then set out on the five-mile walk to Elgin. At the church, Craig produced the counterfeit notes from under a pile of bricks, pretending that his assistant, Jake Yelverson, had hidden them as ordered. Although Pinkerton knew that Yelverson did not exist—he had seen Craig secrete the packet himself—he said nothing. After buying the bills, Allan tucked them in his pocket and, as he did so, was tempted to become a criminal.

Describing his first case many years later, Pinkerton admitted, ". . . a thousand thoughts of sudden wealth and a life free of grinding labor" flashed through his mind. However, as quickly as the temptation appeared it vanished. Yet the famous detective never forgot it and he once wrote: "That with this struggle in my memory, while I have always been unshaken in my determination to never lose sight of a criminal when it once became my duty to pursue him, I can never think of one undergoing the first great temptation to crime, whether he has resisted or fallen, without a touch of genuine human sympathy."

Although Allan had his proof that Craig was a counterfeiter, he knew that his evidence was worthless. There was no witness and, if he took Craig to court, all the latter had to do was deny the whole transaction. Therefore, before they parted, Pinkerton asked the counterfeiter to meet him at the Sauganash Hotel in Chicago, the following week, with four thousand dollars' worth of bogus bills. Craig said he would be there.

Hunt and Bosworth were quite upset when Pinkerton told them what he had done. They were positive that Craig would not keep the appointment. This meant there was no chance of arresting him and recovering the money they had given Allan to buy counterfeit notes. However, Pinkerton finally convinced them that everything would work out, explaining how he planned to have Craig arrested as he passed the worthless money. "That way he won't be able to get away with anything," he confidently told the merchants.

In Chicago, Pinkerton swore out a warrant for Craig's arrest and took two constables with him to the designated hotel. He met Craig in the lobby, but the counterfeiter—who had evidently been watching Allan's movements all day—bluntly denied knowing him and refuted with indignation the charge that he dealt in worthless money. Stunned, Pinkerton ordered the constables to arrest the fellow. Craig was marched off to jail, but when he was searched, no counterfeit notes were found. Nevertheless, after a preliminary hearing, the authorities ordered him held. However, before his case came to trial, Craig "mysteriously escaped," thanks to bribery.

While Allan realized that he had been careless in letting Craig shadow him, his greatest concern was the loss his good and trusting friends, Hunt and Bosworth, had suffered, so he went to George Smith and told him the whole story.

The dour banker listened silently until he had finished his account and then barked, "Listen to me! You were not authorized to do the work and you have no right to a cent. However, I'll pay—but mind you—if you ever work for me again without being told, I'll not give you a penny!"

Pinkerton gladly took the money—and the warning. The former he gave to his friends in Dundee, the latter he kept constantly in mind. Never again was he to act as a detective unless he had been definitely engaged to do so and a fee had been agreed upon in advance.

* * *

Despite the fact that Allan had failed in his attempt to help convict Craig of selling counterfeit money, his attempt added greatly to his reputation. Sheriff Yates swore him in as a deputy and he performed his duties so well that William Church, sheriff of Cook County, asked him to come to Chicago as a member of his staff. Pinkerton accepted the offer, making arrangements with his foreman to run the cooperage. However, he soon was so busy investigating burglaries, shootings, stabbings and robberies that he had no time for barrels and casks. So in 1858 he sold the shop to his foreman and moved to Chicago with his wife and his son William, who was born April 7, 1846.

Pinkerton found Chicago far more exciting than Dundee and thoroughly enjoyed being a lawman. Nevertheless, he often wished he was back on the banks of the Fox. One of the main reasons was because he could not take such an active part in the workings of the Underground Railroad—the secret organization that helped slaves escape from the South to Canada in spite of the Fugitive Slave Law that stated runaway slaves had to be returned to their masters. Allan's cooperage had been a "station" on the railroad and he had furnished shelter, food and clothing to dozens of slaves. Whenever possible, he had

taught them cooperage so that they could earn a living as
free men.

However, in the days to come, Allan Pinkerton was to
do more for the abolition of slavery than he had ever done
as the "Only and Original Cooper of Dundee."

WE NEVER SLEEP

"I established law and justice in the land."
—Hammurabi

CHICAGO WAS BOOMING. Thanks to its geographical location, it had become the largest city in the Midwest, and merchants were proudly boasting that, in a very few years, their town would be much bigger than New York City. It appeared as if they could be right. New construction was going on everywhere, while the tonnage of goods loaded on the Lake Michigan docks for shipment east by way of the Erie Canal increased weekly. A tremendous amount of freight entered and left the city by rail, also. Nearly one hundred trains arrived or departed every day.

Unfortunately, crime flourished as well as business. Pickpockets, sneak thieves, housebreakers and holdup men preyed upon honest citizens, while burglars raided stores, wharves and banks. The city had no regular police force, but depended upon nine constables to keep law and order among a population of 30,000. While it was impossible for

19

either these men or Allan Pinkerton to dam the crime
wave that engulfed Chicago, the latter became well-
known to respectable citizens and criminals alike because
of the number of arrests he made.

Pinkerton's bravery and constant attention to his duty
led to his appointment as a special agent for the United
States Post Office Department. In this capacity, he investigated for the government cases of fraud, extortion
and blackmail involving use of the mail. When Chicago
disbanded its inadequate constable corps and established
a regular police department, Pinkerton was asked to join
the force. He did so, becoming the city's first and only
detective.

In his new post, Allan Pinkerton paid particular attention to bank and railroad robberies. Because of his keen
eyes, which picked up clues that other men would miss,
his great intuitive sense and an uncanny faculty for detecting signs of guilt when questioning a suspect, he was
most successful. Yet, although he enjoyed his work and
was justifiably proud of his record, after debating the matter for some time, he decided to resign from the police
department in 1850. His main reason for doing so was a
simple one. He needed to earn more money, now that his
four-year-old son, William, had a brother and sister—twins
named Joan and Robert—and was convinced that the best
way he could do so was to become a private investigator.

Incidentally, Joan Pinkerton had nothing to say about
naming her children. Allan had their names all picked out
before they were born. His daughter once said, "My dear
little mother never had any choice in naming us—my father announced the name of the new arrival and that
ended the matter."

A cautious man, before resigning, Allan had asked various officials of the Rock Island and Illinois Central

Railroads with whom he had become friendly while investigating thefts from their companies what they thought of his plan. All of them thought it an excellent idea and gave him assurances that they would use his services. Therefore, with E. H. Rucker, a Chicago attorney, as a partner, Pinkerton opened one of the first private detective agencies in the world and the only one in Chicago. A year later, in 1851, the partnership was dissolved and Allan Pinkerton assumed full charge of the activities, personally supervising every detail of the operation of Pinkerton's National Detective Agency until the day of his death.

In a day when many law enforcement officers openly associated with criminals and shared their illegal profits, the code of ethics Pinkerton drew up for his organization reflected the honesty and integrity of the man. Among its main points were: a statement that the Pinkerton Agency would accept no gifts—not even rewards that had been offered before a case was accepted; the policy of never representing a defendant without the permission of the prosecuting authorities; notice that the Agency would not compromise with those having stolen property or take divorce cases or knowingly work for one client against another; a promise that the number of operatives assigned to a case would not be increased without the client's consent; and an understanding that daily reports would be submitted, with all expenses itemized. Charges could be estimated in advance because payment was based on a daily fee.

All clients paid the same amount for the Agency's services. It cost three dollars a day to hire an ordinary operative, eight dollars for a supervisor, while Pinkerton himself received twelve dollars.

From the day he started Pinkerton's National Detective Agency, Allan was fortunate in his assistants, having a

happy faculty for picking the right man for each assignment. He also displayed great skill in turning inexperi-
enced men and women into outstanding detectives. A just
but stern employer, Allan had strict rules for his employees. They could not have "addiction to drink, smoking,
card playing, low dives or use slang." Moreover, he insisted that they wear "somber dress."

We Never Sleep was the slogan Pinkerton chose to be
imprinted upon the Agency's stationery, bulletins and
signs. These also carried the Pinkerton trademark, an open
eye. Allan took this symbol from a little-known episode in
American history. Philip Schuyler, a general in the Revolution who served in the Continental Congress and was
one of the first two senators from New York State, was
particularly concerned with counterfeiting. This was probably due to the fact that he was the father-in-law of Alexander Hamilton, the first secretary of the treasury.
Schuyler suggested that all colonial paper money be called
in by the newly organized Federal Government and new
bills issued. The new notes, Schuyler maintained, should
bear the legend, "Let the name of the money-maker rot"
and be so designed as to show an open eye in a cloud looking down on a cart containing a coffin and a gallows from
which three counterfeiters hung.

Because Pinkerton used the open eye as a trademark,
criminals, who are quick to bestow nicknames, began to
refer to his firm as "The Eye." In time, the general public
also paid tribute to the Agency's symbol by calling private
detectives "private eyes."

American literature, as well as speech, was influenced
by Pinkerton. Until newspapers began to publish lurid
accounts of his captures of wanted men, there was scant
interest in detective stories. Even the well-plotted and
brilliantly written crime tales of Edgar Allan Poe, which

are now considered classics, failed to attract the attention of readers when they first appeared. However, as more and more publicity was given to Pinkerton's National Detective Agency, George P. Munro conceived the idea of using its founder as the central character in a series of stories crammed with violent action and filled with continuous suspense, in which evil was always punished. No dime novels were ever more successful than these yarns about "Old Sleuth" which were inspired by Pinkerton's skill as a detective. "Sleuth," incidentally, is an old Scotch word for the trail left by a man or beast and it, too, has passed into American-English as a synonym for detective.

Actually, it was extremely difficult to make the fictional "Old Sleuth" as clever, colorful and competent as Allan Pinkerton. Fond of disguising himself, he maintained a large collection of costumes and wigs. Yet, despite his great ability to assume the appearance of a workman, minister, farmer or sailor, he had some narrow escapes when trailing dangerous criminals. None, however, was closer than his experience on April 21, 1855, while walking through Chicago's North Side dressed in his own clothes. A riot had broken out and pistols were being discharged on every street corner. Luckily, no one was wounded, but the *Democrat* reported to its readers that Pinkerton narrowly escaped "being shot by a policeman who had become crazy with the excitement of the scene."

While Allan would usually methodically evaluate all the evidence in a case and spend hours looking for clues, he frequenty acted on a hunch. One morning, while taking a walk, he passed a man on the street and immediately came to the conclusion that, in spite of the stranger's respectable appearance, he was a criminal. "As is customary with me," Pinkerton later wrote, "I resolved on immediate action." Because he had noticed that the man "sometimes looked stealthily around and behind him, as if to ascertain if he were being watched or followed," the detective thought it best to disguise himself. Darting into a clothing store owned by a friend, he threw off his dark coat and slipped into a light-colored one and, at the same time, exchanged his fashionable hat for a broad-brimmed sombrero. Then he hastened after the suspect, who entered the Waverly House. Pinkerton followed and learned that the man was registered as John H. Harmon of St. Louis.

While the name meant nothing to Allan—who had a marvelous memory for names, aliases and faces—he still felt there was something suspicious about the fellow. Concealing himself in a doorway, he waited for Harmon to reappear, but, eventually, all the lights were put out in the hotel, so he went home to bed. Early the next morning, he drew a pair of patched pants and a tattered shirt from the Agency wardrobe and set out for the Waverly House. Always observant, Allan had noticed that street repairs were being made in front of the hotel and he was sure that his outfit gave him the appearance of a laborer.

Pinkerton was busy with a trowel when Harmon came out of the Waverly House. Followed by the detective, the suspect went to the railroad station. Here he bought a ticket, then strolled along the sandy shore of Lake Michigan. As Allan watched, Harmon suddenly stooped, dug about in the sand, uncovered a number of watches, rings and other jewelry, stuffed them into his pockets, then walked briskly back to the station and boarded a train. Pinkerton was right behind him. When Harmon sat down, Allan came up behind him, placed a hand on his shoulder and sternly said, "You're under arrest!"

Harmon pushed aside Pinkerton's hand and lunged at the detective shouting, "Help! Help! I'm being robbed!"

His fellow passengers, after taking one look at Pinker-

Disguised as a construction worker, Allan Pinkerton captures a thief.

ton, rushed to his aid. The conductor stopped the train
and asked a young man to fetch a policeman.

"Never mind the police," snapped Allan, who had his
arm locked about Harmon's neck. "Just take the handcuffs
out of my pocket and put them on this crook!"

Pinkerton's tone of command and the handcuffs convinced everyone that Harmon was not being robbed, as he
claimed, and Allan soon had him in jail. When searched,
Harmon's pockets yielded a large sum of money and a
considerable amount of jewelry. Leaving his prisoner
locked in a cell, the detective went back to the Waverly
House and found it almost impossible to walk through the
lobby. Many of the guests were milling around, demanding that the manager find the person who had robbed
them. Welcoming the chance to escape their irate demands, the distraught hotel manager rushed over to Pinkerton, yelling, "Get out! This hotel doesn't admit tramps."

Allan was delighted. Obviously, his disguise was perfect, for he was a personal friend of the manager. Taking
off his battered hat, he apologetically mumbled, "Easy
now, sir; please sir, easy. I'm only here 'cause the policeman at the jail gave me a dime to come and say if anybody here is missing anything anywhere, they'll find it
over there."

While the overjoyed guests rushed to recover their
stolen property, the detective went home. William and
Robert were delighted to see a tramp open the front door
of their house and make himself at home.

Mrs. Pinkerton was not delighted. "Allan," she cried,
"take off those dirty clothes at once!"

✧   ✧   ✧

Besides tracking down train robbers, Allan Pinkerton
also set up security measures for the railroads he served.

His protective methods were so successful that many law-breakers hesitated to rob a line which had been placed in the care of "The Pinks." This led to increased business for the Agency and brought its head into close contact with some of the leading lawyers, financiers, bankers and businessmen of the United States. He became a personal friend of many of them, particularly with two men who were to play a most important part in his life—Abraham Lincoln, then counsel for the Illinois Central Railroad, and its president, George B. McClellan.

Busy as he was with his railroad and bank clients, Allan Pinkerton's services were always available to others who needed them. Thus, in 1857, when a volcano of crime erupted in Chicago—fifty-three burglaries being reported in a single week—the *Tribune* suggested in an editorial that a mass meeting of citizens be held to vote to employ Allan Pinkerton to clean up the city. This was not done, but a group of church officials hired Pinkerton to stop vandalism in the "Old French Cemetery," where graves had been desecrated and headstones thrown over.

Pinkerton assigned eight men, under the direction of Timothy Webster, who was to become one of the Union's most famous spies during the War Between the States, to guard the burying ground. Because there was no way of telling if the members of this detail were alert and at their posts, as strict silence had to be maintained, Allan devised a unique method by which Webster could communicate with his crew. He attached heavy twine to stakes and ordered his chief assistant to drive them in the ground, about three feet apart, when he went on duty and to station his men between them. Every three minutes, Webster was to pull sharply on the line and, when the operative at the next post felt the tug, he was to jerk the twine in turn, until the last man was reached. After a minute's pause, the same signal was to be repeated in reverse order.

Pinkerton carefully picked the crew for this assignment, as he realized that spending night after night in a graveyard, without talking, was far from pleasant. Nevertheless, after being on duty for several weeks, some of the men frankly admitted that they were frightened and asked to be relieved—but not so a certain young man named O'Grady. He bragged loudly of his bravery and told tall tales of his adventures in Ireland while chasing witches and goblins through the night. However, Pinkerton, always a shrewd judge of men, realized that O'Grady was only boasting to conceal the fact that he was fearful of what might happen during his long tour of duty in the cemetery. Allan, who delighted in practical jokes, could not resist the temptation to see what would happen if the braggart's courage were put to a test, and he decided to have some fun with the young man.

After letting it be known that he had been called out of town, Pinkerton went to the cemetery by a roundabout route and hid in some bushes close to O'Grady's post, before his men arrived. A bit before the "witching" hour of midnight he covered himself with a sheet and, wailing like a banshee, rushed toward his victim. Without waiting to jerk the twine and give the alarm, O'Grady dashed off in the opposite direction, screeching wildly, with the "ghost" close behind. Scampering for the cemetery fence, the frightened man cleared it easily. Allan had no intention of following, but the other operatives, aroused by O'Grady's yells of terror, began firing their pistols. Realizing his danger, Pinkerton, despite the handicap of the sheet, also cleared the fence and ran as fast as possible across the open prairie. O'Grady, looking over his shoulder, thought he was still being pursued by a ghost, and put on more speed. When he reached the bank of the Chicago River, he plunged in, swam to the opposite shore, scrambled out and continued his flight.

Laughing heartily, despite the fact that his joke might have had serious consequences both to O'Grady and himself, Pinkerton shed his ghostly robes, plodded miles back to the city, took a room in a hotel for the remainder of the night and was seated calmly at his desk the next morning, waiting for Webster to hand in his report, which he accepted, "ghost" and all—to the operative's amazement—without a single word of comment.

Having had his fun, Allan wanted to make amends. He advertised for O'Grady in newspapers throughout the country, but never picked up a single clue to his whereabouts. "So far as I know," he once said, "O'Grady is still running."

"Let no guilty man escape, if it can be avoided."
—Grant

Pinkerton thoughtfully reread a telegram he had just received.

CAN YOU SEND ME A MAN HALF HORSE AND HALF ALLI-
GATOR I HAVE GOT "BIT" ONCE MORE. WHEN CAN YOU SEND
HIM

E. S. SANFORD, V.P.

ADAMS EXPRESS COMPANY

Allan lit a cigar and sent for the file containing the Agency's correspondence with E. S. Sanford, relative to a theft in the Montgomery, Alabama, office of the Adams Express Company. Actually, Allan did not need the file, he knew what it contained. In the fall of 1858, Sanford had written him detailing the circumstances in the case. Ten thousand dollars, being shipped to a bank in Columbus, Georgia, had mistakenly been placed in the messenger's pouch on the Atlanta-Montgomery route. The

pouch also contained another packet of mis-sent bills totaling about five thousand dollars. Maroney, the company's local agent in the latter city, had forwarded the
second package to the correct address, but swore he had
never seen the other bills. Chase, the express messenger,
also claimed he knew nothing about the missing money.
He stated that he had stored the pouch in a locked safe
on boarding the train in Atlanta and had delivered it upon
arriving in Montgomery. What, Sanford had asked, was
Pinkerton's theory on the case?

In his answer, Allan had reported that he had checked
the routine observed by the express company in handling
money shipments and, as a result, was convinced that
either Maroney or Chase, or both of them, were guilty of
the theft. Of the two, Pinkerton was inclined to accuse
Maroney, as money pouches were locked by the agent in
the city from which they were shipped and unlocked by
the agent at the delivery point, both men being watched
by the messenger, who had no key to the pouch. In order
for Chase alone to steal the money, Pinkerton had explained, he would have to cut the pouch in transit or
knock out Maroney and steal the key. As the pouch was
unharmed and the agent had not been the subject of an
attack, Allan was convinced Maroney was responsible for
the crime. However, the detective frankly admitted that,
even if he went to Montgomery and gathered enough evidence to prove his theory, he doubted that he could convict the agent because of the strong feeling against
Northerners in slave-holding states.

To Pinkerton's great disappointment, Sanford had not
replied to his letter and asked the Agency to investigate
the theft, for Allan was most anxious to add the Adams
firm to his list of clients.

Founded in 1839 by Alvin Adams, a produce merchant

who had failed in the Panic of 1837, to carry packages, letters and valuables between Boston and Worcester, Massachusetts, the concern now served much of the United States. Meanwhile, Adams, who had recouped his fortune, had invested heavily in railroad stock and was a director of several lines. Pinkerton felt that, if he satisfactorily completed an investigation for the express company, its owner would recommend his services whenever they might be needed by the railroads in which he had financial interests.

Despite the fact that Sanford had shown no intention of hiring Pinkerton, the detective had not lost interest in the case. He had learned that the express company, its reputation for security endangered, was actively investigating the theft, without success. Maroney had been shadowed while on vacation in Virginia, where he had spent so much money his employers decided to discharge him, although they had no proof he was spending stolen money. When told of this decision, Maroney offered to resign, effective the day his successor reported for duty. The company agreed, but, before the new agent arrived, forty thousand dollars disappeared from a pouch Maroney had prepared in Chase's presence for the messenger to carry from Montgomery to Atlanta. There was no question that the money had been placed in the pouch before Maroney locked it—Chase had signed a receipt for the pouch, which he would not have done had he not seen the missing money packed by Maroney.

Pinkerton did not send one man in answer to Sanford's telegram asking for help. He marshaled the entire forces of the Agency. His handling of his first investigation for the Adams Express Company was a typical example of the teamwork, resourcefulness and careful planning that made "The Eye" feared by wrong-doers. Operatives went into action in places as far apart as Alabama and New York City. One got a job as a desk-clerk in the hotel where Maroney and his wife lived. Another, dressed in clothes purchased at a church rummage sale, disguised himself as an immigrant German and followed Maroney by rail and steamboat from Montgomery to New Orleans and back.

Allan also went to Montgomery, himself. This was a courageous move. The fuse which was to explode the War Between the States was sputtering loudly and Pinkerton was a well-known abolitionist. Moreover, his friendship with Elijah Lovejoy, John Brown and other antislavery leaders made him unpopular in the South. An avid reader, Pinkerton added to the hazards of his journey by taking along a copy of Dickens' *Martin Chuzzlewit*—which contains strong statements against slavery—to read on the train. However, he wisely tossed the book out the window as the locomotive chugged through the quiet Virginia countryside.

While gathering evidence in Montgomery, Pinkerton received a coded telegram from one of his operatives, stating that Maroney's wife was visiting her brother-in-law in Jenkintown, Pennsylvania, a small town near Philadelphia. Allan immediately ordered Kate Warne to go there. Mrs. Warne, the first woman in the United States to become a detective, had had great difficulty persuading Pinkerton to employ her, but had developed into an outstanding operative. In two years she had risen to the rank of superintendent of what Pinkerton's National Detective Agency called its "female department."

Allan's instructions to Mrs. Warne were simple. She was to pose as Madame Imbert, the wife of a jailed forger, and become friendly with Mrs. Maroney. He also took steps to provide her with male companionship. From his agents'

reports, Pinkerton knew that Mrs. Maroney enjoyed dancing and the theater, so he made sure she would have no
difficulty securing an escort for these pleasures. He requested Sanford to assign a young, handsome "employee"
with a pleasing personality to the Adams Express Company office in Jenkintown—all the Agency's men with the
necessary qualifications being engaged on other cases—
where he was to cultivate the lady socially "at the company's expense."

Sanford's choice, Arthur De Forest, soon forgot he was
playing a part and fell in love with Mrs. Maroney. Before
long, he noticed that everywhere they went, a man loitered nearby, making it impossible for them to be alone.
Finally, De Forest hailed a constable. "Arrest that man,"
he demanded; "he follows us everywhere." Detective Rivers, who had been shadowing the pair, went to jail and it
took the combined efforts of both Pinkerton and Sanford
to get him released.

Back in Montgomery, the operative posing as a hotel
clerk had stored a trunk for the former express agent and
reported to Pinkerton that he was positive the stolen
money was cached in it. Therefore, Operative Porter was
stunned when Maroney told him he was going north to
see his wife, but was leaving the trunk behind. This news
was quickly wired to Pinkerton, who was now directing
his operatives from the Agency's New York office, and he
decided to arrest Maroney upon his arrival in that city.

The suspect had no idea that among his fellow passengers on the New York-New Jersey ferry were a United
States Marshal, a lawyer representing the Adams Express
Company, and a Pinkerton agent. None of the three had
ever seen Maroney, but they had his picture. While in
New Orleans, the suspect had gone to the barber's, had
his hair cut in a new style, his beard trimmed and then

went to a photographer's and had his picture taken. The operative who was following him went into the photography shop the next day, passed himself off as a friend of Maroney's, purchased a copy of the picture as a "keepsake" and mailed it to the Agency. It was an excellent likeness and the trio on the ferry recognized Maroney immediately. Loudly protesting his innocence, Maroney was hauled off to jail. His bail was later set at $100,000.

Pinkerton had arranged for one of his agents named White, who pretended to be an embezzler, to share Maroney's cell. The detective lavishly tipped the jailers, so they allowed him visitors at any hour and the privilege of having his nephew (actually another Pinkerton agent) bring his meals in from a nearby restaurant. Maroney was delighted when his cellmate insisted that he share his food and invited him to "ask the boy to do your errands." Not only was prison fare most unappetizing, but, more important, he now had a way to smuggle letters by the guards. Little did he know that, before they were mailed, Allan Pinkerton carefully steamed them open, copied their contents, resealed the envelopes and then sent them on to their destination.

Meanwhile, Mrs. Maroney was vainly trying to raise her husband's bail. She discussed the problem with her dear friend, Madame Imbert, but although that lady was most sympathetic, she had no practical suggestions. She did, however, have one for Pinkerton. "Mrs. Maroney planning a trip to Montgomery—make sure she is shadowed," she wired him.

She was shadowed—most carefully. Although watched constantly, she spoke to no one during her entire journey and, on arriving in Montgomery, went directly to the hotel where the trunk was stored. Porter, warned of her coming, offered to help her find the trunk and open it, but

Mrs. Maroney refused his aid and insisted upon entering the hotel's storage room alone. She carried no bundle when she came out, but the keen-eyed operative noticed that her bustle seemed quite large for a lady-of-fashion and passed his observation on to his superior. Nor did the bustle get any smaller on the trip back to Jenkintown, according to the detective who watched her during the return trip.

Upon arriving at the Philadelphia suburb, Mrs. Maroney asked Madame Imbert, who had gone to the station to meet her, where she hid her valuables. "When I have any," replied the quick-thinking Mrs. Warne, "I bury them in the cellar or in the garden."

WE NEVER SLEEP

"Everything comes if a man will only wait."
—Disraeli

ALTHOUGH PINKERTON OPERATIVES WATCHED the garden day and night, not a spadeful of earth was turned. Nevertheless, when Mrs. Maroney went shopping wearing the same dress she had traveled in coming back from Montgomery, the bustle was noticeably smaller.

"Not in the garden, not in the bustle," Allan mused, "then there's something in the cellar. Search it!"

It was fortunate that Mrs. Warne was visiting Mrs. Maroney the night Operative Rivers decided to sneak into the cellar and look for the stolen money. While he was crawling over the dirt floor, looking for signs of freshly shoveled earth, he unknowingly backed into a pile of boxes. They fell with a resounding crash. Rivers managed to wiggle out of a window and escape because Mrs. Warne, sensing what had happened, led the pursuit in the wrong direction. When she was sure her associate was safe, Mrs. Warne led the way downstairs to the cellar.

Spotting the open window, she quickly closed it without being observed, then deftly persuaded Mrs. Maroney that the boxes had merely toppled over.

Meanwhile, George H. Bangs, Pinkerton's chief assistant, was pretending to be the lawyer of the operative "planted" in Maroneys' cell. Bangs gravely assured his pseudo client that he would shortly be released, and he acted the part of a man with powerful political connections so well that Maroney, growing more and more desperate, asked him to take his case. "Get me extradited to Alabama," he begged. "I have good friends there and will never be convicted."

Maroney readily admitted to Bangs that he had stolen from his employers. He explained that the first theft was very simple. The package of bills was mislabeled and he knew it never could be traced. However, he lost the entire ten thousand dollars betting on horse races and speculating in cotton. Maroney also told Bangs that he had taken the forty thousand dollars now being sought. It had not been difficult to drop the packages containing the bills past the pouch opening and let them fall behind the counter. Chase was so busy signing waybills that he paid no attention and put his signature on the required receipt without question. When Bangs asked Maroney where the money was, he evaded giving a direct answer and merely stated that, until his wife's trip to Montgomery, the bills had been hidden between layers of cigars in a stored trunk.

Bangs listened carefully and "sympathetically" to Maroney's story and then assured him that he would do everything he could to get him sent to Alabama. Before leaving the cell, he turned to his fellow agent and briskly said, "I'll have you out of here in an hour. Don't you worry. That goes for you too, Mr. Maroney. I'm taking a great deal of interest in your case."

He certainly did. Writing a detailed report to Pinkerton, Bangs summarized Maroney's confession, but ruefully admitted that he had failed to find out exactly where the stolen money was now hidden. Bangs really had no need to worry. As soon as he had left the jail, Maroney turned to his cellmate and asked, "How'd you like to make fifteen thousand dollars?"

"I'd like it fine. What do I have to do?"

"Figure some way to get a duplicate Adams Express Company key and plant it on that fellow Chase I've told you about, along with four thousand dollars. Then, have him arrested. My lawyer won't have any trouble proving I'm innocent with that kind of evidence. Everyone will think Chase stole the money."

"That's a clever scheme, Maroney. You can count me in on it."

"I counted you in on this a long time ago, pal. You're my kind of man and I trust you. Now listen carefully. My wife has the money in a safe place, but I'm afraid, if she tries to take it south, she'll be caught. So I'm writing her a note, telling her to give all the cash to you. When you get it, take out your fifteen thousand and the frame money. Bring the rest to Montgomery. I'll pick it up when I'm released."

Operative White readily agreed to Maroney's proposition. However, once "released" from jail, he was more anxious to get the money than Mrs. Maroney was to give it to him. Perplexed, she appealed to her confidante, Madame Imbert, who advised her to do what her husband wanted. After some hesitation, Mrs. Maroney took the detective to the cellar and, while Mrs. Warne held a flickering kerosene lamp, the agent dug where Mrs. Maroney pointed and unearthed an oilskin pouch. Slipping it into his pocket, White told the ladies not to be concerned and that he would see Maroney in Montgomery very soon. Just as he left the house, a man stepped out from behind a tree. It was Pinkerton. The two detectives set out immediately for the main office of the Adams Express Company. Sanford was waiting and nervously counted out the bills. They totaled $39,515 and the expressman delightedly wrote a receipt for that amount, which Pinkerton carefully placed in his wallet. On returning to Chicago, he had it framed and hung it over his desk.

In order to keep Mrs. Maroney under surveillance during her husband's trial, Madame Imbert invited her to be a guest in a charming house in Chicago she said she had purchased with money given to her by her forger husband before he was jailed. What Mrs. Maroney did not know was that her hostess, as head of the female department of Pinkerton's National Detective Agency, lived in the building, along with all the other women operatives. Their employer maintained this place in order to assure them a comfortable residence. However, the house was vacant when the two ladies arrived. Pinkerton, warned by wire, had secured other accommodations for his "female department."

Despite the fact that Bangs seemed to be having trouble getting him extradited to Alabama, Maroney was not too concerned. Frequent letters from his former cellmate assured him that the money was waiting for him in Montgomery. Therefore, he was not the least bit worried when, at last, he was taken south and ordered to stand trial. As he entered the courtroom, he looked about for his friend. When he did not see him among the spectators, however, Maroney became alarmed, fearing that he had been dou-

ble-crossed at the last minute. Finally, he saw White and
his anxious frown turned to a broad grin when he noticed
his cellmate had taken a seat in the section reserved for
witnesses for the prosecution.

"He's more nervous than I am." Maroney chuckled to
himself—then, when White looked coldly at him, turned
away and leaned over to whisper to the district attorney,
he suddenly realized the truth. When court opened, Maroney pleaded guilty and was sentenced to ten years at
hard labor. Despite her part in the plot, his wife was not
charged with any crime.

*   *   *

Newspapers all over the world published full accounts
of how Pinkerton's National Detective Agency—English
journalists referred to it as America's Scotland Yard—had
solved the Adams Express case. As a result of all this publicity, Allan's organization became recognized as the only
really effective force of detectives, public or private, in
this country. Moreover, when it became known that Pinkerton, following his regulations, had refused the ten-thou-
sand-dollar reward the express firm had offered for the
arrest and conviction of the thief—while his bill for services and expenses was far below that figure—the growth of
the Agency was assured.

Pinkerton was proud of the way Maroney had been
trapped and the case was always one of his favorites. He
wrote a book about it in 1874, entitled, *The Expressman
and the Detectives,* giving all the details of the investigation. He told his readers; "If there be any incidental em-
bellishment, it is so slight that the actors in these scenes
from the drama of life would never themselves detect it;
and if the incidents seem to the reader at all marvelous or

improbable, I can but remind him, in the words of the old adage, that 'Truth is stranger than fiction.' "

* * *

Actually, there was nothing spectacular in the way "The Eye" handled the Adams Express case. After Allan had placed White in Maroney's cell and sent Mrs. Warne to Jenkintown, he and his staff spent their time watching and waiting. Nevertheless, when necessary, Pinkerton's vivid imagination furnished him with fantastic methods for solving a crime.

Among the cases he unraveled by extraordinary means was the murder of a bank cashier in a small Tennessee town. It was a cold trail. Pinkerton was not called in for nearly a year after Jackson Carter's death, but, by talking to policemen, bank employees and others, he learned that when the bank opened for business, the cashier's body, his head badly battered, had been found in front of the vault, where he slept every night. Allan also picked up the information that the bank's rear door had been forced open and the officers had discovered a half-burned promissory note, signed by Carter's best friend, Slocum, in the ashes of the fireplace.

"Slocum," the bank president informed the detective, "hasn't been the same since Carter was killed. He wouldn't even look at his chum's body and, although he used to come in here several times a day, he hasn't entered the bank since the murder. Isn't that strange?"

Pinkerton nodded his agreement, but with mental reservations. Slocum wasn't acting strangely for a man with a guilty conscience. "Perhaps," the detective muttered to himself, "I can give his conscience some help."

Upon learning that Slocum was seeking a married couple as servants, Allan was able to plant a trustworthy man and wife, Mr. and Mrs. Binney, in his home. As they went about their duties, the pair connected one of Pinkerton's inventions—a speaking tube similar to those now used in the foyers of apartment houses—from their employer's bed in a first-floor room to an opening bored in the outside wall behind a bush. Meanwhile, Operative Green, who had accompanied Pinkerton, while chatting with the local druggist, picked up the important information that Jackson Carter had been fond of toilet water. Pinkerton sent his assistant to buy a bottle of the brand Carter liked best and gave it to the Binneys, with orders to sprinkle it on Slocum's clothes and handkerchiefs. He also gave them a bottle of red dyed water and told them to use it to sprinkle the letters J. C. on Slocum's pillows.

It was Pinkerton's firm conviction that a criminal's "crime haunts him continually, and the burden of concealment becomes at last too heavy to bear alone. It must find a voice . . . he must relieve himself of the terrible secret which is bearing him down." Therefore, their superior kept suggesting to the Binneys new ways to upset their employer who had, the detective was positive, killed the cashier.

"We keep him awake half the night, groaning at him through the tube, Mr. Pinkerton," Binney reported a week later. "During the day, we don't see much of him as he spends most of the time in the library with the door locked. My wife thinks he sits in there and broods."

"I think she's right," replied Pinkerton. "Try to keep an eye on him at all times, for we don't want him to leave town unless he is followed. Meanwhile, make those groans more ghastly."

Two days later, Allan Pinkerton was awakened by a frantic pounding on his hotel room door. It was pitch-black and he fumbled for several minutes before he found a match to light the lamp. Upon opening the door, Binney rushed in and breathlessly gasped that he had just discovered that Slocum had spent the night packing and was planning to leave on the ten-minutes-past-five train. Pinkerton quickly glanced at his watch—it was two minutes past five! He pounded on the wall to rouse Green in the next room, and began dressing. Coatless and tucking their shirts in as they dashed toward the station, which, fortunately, was close by, the two detectives scrambled aboard the train just as it was pulling away.

When Green finally caught his breath, he asked, "Now what? Neither of us has ever seen Slocum."

"First, let's find out how many passengers got on at the last stop," answered Pinkerton and went looking for the conductor. When he returned, he told Green that three men had boarded the train. One was obviously a farmer on his way to spend the day in the city. "Here's how we'll find out which one of the other two is Slocum," he explained. "Hold my handkerchief while I douse it with the scent Carter used. I stuck a bottle of it in my pocket while I was dressing. . . . Fine—that's enough. We'll try that man next to the fourth window on the right-hand side first. Take the seat behind him and give me time to get up to the front of the car, then wave my handkerchief back and forth. I'll watch his reactions."

Green merely flicked the handkerchief two or three times when the man jumped to his feet, stared wildly about, pushed his seat companion roughly aside, rushed toward the door and frantically tugged at the handle.

"Here, let me help," offered the detective, skillfully getting in his way.

Suddenly, Slocum smelled the toilet water Allan had sprinkled on the lapel of his coat. With a cry of terror the man knocked Pinkerton across the aisle, threw open the door and leaped from the platform. Staggering to his feet, Allan pulled the emergency cord and, when the hand-brakes were set, the train ground to a stop. Crewmen and passengers rushed back along the right-of-way to where Slocum lay. To their amazement, he was babbling of initials written in blood, groans in the night and the smell of scent. Then, realizing he was dying, the injured man confessed that he had killed his friend Carter because he could not meet the note he had signed.

"Sometimes," Pinkerton remarked somberly to Green as he handed him a cigar, "a guilty consicence is a detective's best friend."

* * *

A coded telegram lay on Allan's desk when he returned to Chicago. It informed him that his good friend John Brown, who often spent the night at the Pinkerton home on Adams Street, was in serious trouble. Perhaps the most celebrated of all abolitionists, Brown, hoping that the slaves in Virginia would rebel against their masters, had seized the Federal armory and arsenal at Harpers Ferry, in order to secure arms for their revolt. Now Brown and his eighteen followers were being besieged by a force of United States Marines under the direction of Colonel Robert E. Lee. As there was no doubt that the veteran of "Bloody Kansas" would be captured and sentenced to be executed, Pinkerton was asked to use all the resources of his organization and rescue Brown while he was in prison awaiting trial.

For once, Allan Pinkerton did not know what to do. Loyal to his adopted country, he disliked defying the authorities, but, at the same time, he was a staunch abolitionist, as well as a good friend of Brown's. He had shown this when John Brown, aided by a band of armed men, had raided plantations in Mississippi, liberated a number of slaves and then set out for Canada, treking across Iowa and Illinois in the dead of winter. When the hungry, half-frozen party reached Chicago, Pinkerton, despite being an officer of the law, had ignored the Fugitive Slave Act and hidden the men and their horses, provided food and shelter for them and eventually secured sufficient funds to send the band on to Detroit. This was not the first time the detective had aided Brown, and he was proud of their association.

"John Brown was my bosom friend; and more than one dark night found us working earnestly together in behalf of the fleeing bondsman, who was striving for his liberty," he wrote later.

After pondering what to do about his fellow abolitionist, Allan decided to go to Charleston, Virginia, where Brown was imprisoned. Pinkerton took some of his best operatives with him, calling them in from various cases. Disguised as a southern planter, Allan had no difficulty in becoming friendly with a young officer who had served under Lee at Harpers Ferry. The dashing lieutenant described in detail how Brown was being guarded and outlined the precautions that were to be taken on the day of his hanging. A few years later, Pinkerton often wished that Jeb Stuart, then a leading Confederate general, still gave military information so freely to strangers. It would have made Allan's job as head of the Federal Secret Service far more simple.

After carefully considering all the facts, Pinkerton reluctantly came to the conclusion that not even his operatives could free Brown. "My efforts in his behalf were unceasing and had it not been for the excessive watchfulness of those having him in charge, the pages of American history would never have been stained with a record of his execution," he stated years later. At the time, Allan glumly ordered his men to return to their previous assignments, and he set out for Chicago with a heavy heart. Pinkerton would not have been so discouraged, as well as so unhappy had he but known that he was about to play a major role in one of the most exciting episodes in the history of the United States.

"We first survey the plot . . . "
—Shakespeare

W HILE VAST NUMBERS of Americans greeted the arrival of 1861 with bells, whistles, toasts and cheers, many people on both sides of the Mason-Dixon line saw no reason to celebrate because they felt the nation faced the most crucial year in its history since the days of the American Revolution. The success of the recently organized Republican Party in electing Abraham Lincoln president could very well mean the end of the United States. The lanky lawyer from Illinois had made his position on slavery clear in his debates with Douglas: "A house divided against itself cannot stand. I believe that this government cannot endure half slave and half free." If Southerners interpreted this statement to mean that Lincoln was planning to use Federal authority to stamp out slavery, there was little doubt that his inaugural would lead to secession.

Lincoln's election delighted Pinkerton. The two had

been friendly for years, ever since their first meeting while
Allan was investigating robberies for the Illinois Central
Railroad, for which Lincoln was counsel. Moreover, the
detective, as an abolitionist, thoroughly approved of the
Republicans' aim to prevent the extension of slavery in
any new states formed out of the Northwest Territory.

Both from personal observation and the reports of his
operatives who had worked on cases in the South, Pinkerton knew that the Lincoln administration faced difficult
times. However, he had no idea of the extent of the unrest
in slave-holding states until early in January, 1861, when,
in reply to an urgent telegram, he went east to confer with
Samuel M. Felton, president of the Philadelphia, Wilmington and Baltimore Railroad. At the time, this road
was the only direct line connecting New York City and
New England with Washington.

Felton worriedly explained to the detective that there
were rumors that secessionist agitators were planning to
destroy the bridges belonging to the railroad in Maryland.
This would, of course, cut Washington off from the Northern States. After checking Felton's evidence, Allan agreed
that it would be wise to set up security measures along
the right-of-way and he undertook to furnish the necessary
protection.

Pinkerton sent to Chicago for a detachment of agents
and, when they arrived, began an investigation of the supposed plot against the railroad. Although he and his men
visited every community in which a bridge belonging to
the line was located, they could not unearth any evidence
that Felton had cause for worry. However, Pinkerton left
an operative in each town to continue the inquiry. Because Allan heard extremely bitter remarks about Lincoln
and the North everywhere he went in Baltimore, he decided to remain in that city himself.

He rented a large house on South Street, to use as a headquarters. He didn't need so many rooms, but its location was ideal. Also, alleys connected the streets in the front and rear of the building, making it possible to enter it on all four sides. Agents slipped in and out of the four doors all night long, to deliver reports and to receive assignments from either Pinkerton or George Bangs, who had left the Agency's New York City office in charge of a subordinate in order to assist his chief. Mrs. Warne had also come to Baltimore, as ordered in a telegram sent to the Agency's Chicago headquarters. After sewing a black-and-white cockade on her clothing—the emblem of secession—she went about the city, gathering information. However, no Pinkerton operative was able to learn of a plan to destroy the bridges. Nevertheless, Pinkerton intuitively felt a conspiracy of some sort was being organized.

On February tenth—one day before Abraham Lincoln was to leave Springfield, Illinois, for his inaugural in Washington—the detective received a letter from the master mechanic of Felton's railroad that proved his hunch correct. "I am informed," Pinkerton read, "that the son of a distinguished citizen of Maryland said that he had taken an oath with others to assassinate Mr. Lincoln before he gets to Washington."

"What do you think of this, Bangs?" asked Pinkerton.

Allan's assistant read the letter quickly, handed it back and replied, "It could be just another rumor like the one about the bridges. No names are given and the writer doesn't offer any proof that the cavalry regiment being formed in Perryman is, as we've heard, really a secret society dedicated to the assassination of Lincoln. Frankly, it doesn't seem—"

"Wait a minute," interrupted Pinkerton. "If you were

planning to murder safely a person traveling by train, how would you do it?"

Bangs hesitated, then grinned sheepishly and admitted, "I should have seen it. Naturally, the best way would be to blow up a bridge while the train was passing over it."

"Of course. The plan is probably to blow up a specific bridge, but someone couldn't keep quiet. Fortunately, he exaggerated and that's how Felton learned his property was in danger and sent for us. Let's hope we're as lucky finding out just what those society horsemen in Perryman really have in mind."

They were extremely lucky, thanks to Timothy Webster. The handsome English-born operative had met Pinkerton while serving as a policeman at the World's Crystal Palace Exposition in New York City and had resigned that post to work for the Agency. Webster was a quiet, reserved individual by nature. Yet, when assigned to an investigation that required him to be sociable, he acted the part of a prince of good fellows to perfection.

"Webster's talent for sustaining a role of this kind," according to Pinkerton, "amounted to positive genius" and he then went on to say that "in a lifetime of detective experience I have never met one who could more readily adapt himself to circumstances." While stationed in Perryman, Webster had become very popular and had convinced everyone that he was an ardent secessionist.

Ordered to return to Perryman and to continue the investigation, Webster was warmly greeted by his friends. He hadn't been in town more than a day when he was invited to join the cavalry regiment that was giving "The Eye" so much concern. Naturally, he accepted and was soon prancing about on a fine horse, as were all the young men of Perryman. One night the captain of the troop took him to a well-guarded house whose windows were covered with blankets. Inside, the feeble glow of a turned-down lamp enabled the detective to recognize a group of his familiar comrades and to note the presence of three strangers. The trio was not introduced, but when the captain signaled them to speak, they gave the hushed gathering the details of a plot to shoot Lincoln in Baltimore's Calvert Street Station on February twenty-third.

As soon as he could, Webster relayed this information to Pinkerton. A few days later, Webster's news was confirmed by Harry Davies, another operative, who had found his task of posing as Joseph H. Ward, son of a wealthy plantation owner, an easy one, since he was well-educated and had lived in New Orleans. Thanks to his personal charm and liberal use of his expense account, Davies had become familiar with a group of radical secessionists and had joined their secret organization. Late one night, after attending a meeting of the group, he hastened to the house on South Street with full details of the assassination plot.

The plan was a simple one and had little chance of failing. As Webster had reported, Lincoln was to be murdered—either stabbed or shot—while changing trains in Baltimore. Marshal Kane, head of the city's police force, was one of the leaders in the conspiracy, so only a small detachment of officers would be detailed to guard Lincoln and to control the expected crowd of curious sight-seers. Kane had arranged that, when a well-staged fight broke out at the far end of the platform, his men, under the pretext of stopping it, would leave their posts, thus allowing the crowd to surge forward. In the confusion, the assassin would kill the president-elect, make his escape, and be taken in a waiting carriage to a chartered Chesapeake Bay steamer, bound for a southern port.

After Davies left, Pinkerton had a long talk with Bangs

and gave him a note for Mrs. Warne. Then, packing his carpetbag, the detective took the early train for Philadelphia and went directly from the station to Felton's office. The railroad executive listened to Allan's account of what he had learned in Baltimore without a single interruption, then simply asked, "What can I do to help prevent this terrible thing?"

"Frankly, I don't know if anybody can do anything as yet," admitted Pinkerton. "I can't get near Lincoln—and he probably wouldn't pay any attention to me if I could. The only member of his party that I know is Norman Judd of Chicago. He's our one hope. Mrs. Warne went to see him yesterday in New York City, to tell him what we'd found out—that is, just that Lincoln's life was in danger —and to warn him to expect a message when he arrives here in Philadelphia tomorrow. If Judd took Mrs. Warne seriously, perhaps we can do something."

The next day, Abraham Lincoln and his traveling companions reached Philadelphia. Throngs lined the streets, cheering and waving flags as carriages carrying the president-elect and his party rolled toward the Continental Hotel. At one intersection, a young man darted out from the sidewalk and handed Judd a slip of paper. It contained a single line of writing:

St. Louis Hotel—J. H. Hutchinson

When Judd arrived at the hotel, he found "Hutchinson" was none other than his old friend Pinkerton, who was fond of using assumed names. Allan introduced Judd to Felton, asked him to sit down and began to read a complete report of the plot to kill Lincoln as compiled by his staff. Before he was halfway through, Judd began to pace up and down the room, frequently pausing to fire a question at the detective.

When Allan had finished reading, Judd slumped in a chair, shook his head and woefully said, "I've known there was strong feeling against the man, but I had no idea that things were this bad. Your evidence is too powerful to ignore, Pinkerton. I'm convinced all that you say is true —but getting Lincoln to agree with us is another matter. There's only one thing to do. Come on, gentlemen, let's go and see him."

It was easier said than done. A solid mass of people blocked the entrance of the Continental Hotel, hoping to catch a glimpse of the president-to-be. The trio pushed, shoved, lost their hats and had buttons torn off their coats, but they could not get through the throng.

Finally, Judd turned to his companions and gasped, "Let's get out of here and see if there's a door in the rear."

Linking arms, they charged through the group of onlookers standing in front of the employees' entrance to the Continental and fought their way to the lobby. Judd hailed one of the military officers who was accompanying Lincoln and he cleared a path for the three men. Breathless and battered, they reached the suite of the president-elect.

Lincoln smiled broadly when he saw their tattered clothes and drawled, "What have you men been doing, fighting wildcats barehanded?"

Judd raised a protesting hand and spoke sharply, "Abe, this is no time for jokes. We've got to talk to you—at once and alone. Wrestling with wildcats is fun compared with the job we've got to do!"

Sensing the seriousness of the situation, Lincoln led the way to his bedroom, closed the door behind his visitors and then asked, "Well, what's wrong?"

"Plenty, Abe, plenty! Just sit down and listen to Pinkerton!"

7

"God bless the train that brought me here."
—Kilmer

W HEN ALLAN FINISHED, Lincoln pushed his chair
back, unwound himself and walked over to the detective saying, "You present a mighty strong case, Pinkerton, but I'd be a pretty poor lawyer if I didn't want to
cross-examine."

"Go right ahead, sir," offered the detective.

After questioning Allan for some time, Lincoln finally
admitted that he could see that his life was endangered
and asked, "What do you think I should do?"

"Go to Washington tonight," replied Pinkerton. "The
assassins won't expect you and you'll be in and out of Baltimore before they can make a move."

"Impossible! I've promised to raise the flag over Inde-
pendence Hall tomorrow morning at sunrise and then go
to Harrisburg in the afternoon and address the legislature.
Those appointments must be kept!"

For over an hour Judd, Felton and Pinkerton argued

with Lincoln, but nothing they said would make him
change his mind. Finally, they agreed that he could follow
his schedule, although Allan warned him, "This is the
only concession you'll get. Just as soon as you're through
speaking in Harrisburg, you must do as you are told. Otherwise, we cannot be responsible for your life. Now, if
you'll excuse us, sir, we have work to do."

Outside the hotel, Pinkerton requested Judd and Felton
to come to his hotel room at midnight. "I'm going to ask
Franciscus of the Pennsylvania Railroad and Sanford to
join us," he informed his friends.

"Why?" demanded Judd. "Are you going to ship Lincoln in a crate by Adams Express?"

Grimly smiling, Allan quickly retorted, "That might not
be such a bad idea. However, Sanford, besides being vice-
president of Adams, is an officer of the American Telegraph Company. With his co-operation, no one will be
able to send a telegram giving news of Lincoln's movements—for I'm sure he's being watched by spies."

Sanford was willing to co-operate, but it was five in the
morning before the group, under Pinkerton's direction,
worked out a satisfactory plan to protect the president-
elect. An hour later, Lincoln raised Old Glory over Inde-
pendence Hall and, after a brief speech, boarded the train
for Harrisburg. On the way, he read the mail that had
been delivered to his private car. Among the letters were
frantic notes from William G. Seward, who was to become
Lincoln's secretary of state, and General Winfield Scott,
hero of the Mexican War, popularly called "Old Fuss and
Feathers" because he insisted that his soldiers' uniforms
be spotless, even on the battlefield. Both men warned Lincoln that they had heard of a plot to assassinate him.

After reading the letters, Lincoln requested everyone
to leave the car except Judd. When they were alone, Lin-

coln handed his friend the letters and dryly commented, "Seems as if Pinkerton knew what he was talking about. What are his plans?"

Judd didn't know what to say. Pinkerton, fearful that their scheme might become known to the conspirators, had warned him not to discuss their plans with anyone until the last possible moment. To cover his confusion, he replied, "Plans? Oh, yes, our detective friend is tending to them right now in Philadelphia."

"What plans, Judd?" Lincoln insisted.

"Well, you'll have to know sooner or later, so I'll tell you. According to your schedule, after speaking to the legislature, you're to be guest of honor at a dinner given by Governor Curtin. Then, after a public reception, you're supposed to spend the night at the executive mansion. But, instead of staying in Harrisburg, you're leaving for Washington tonight."

Pinkerton, knowing that the dinner was to begin at five o'clock, had hoped that Lincoln would be able to leave the place by six. It was impossible. A tremendous throng crowded the banquet hall, anxious to shake the president-elect's hand and wish him good luck.

At last, Curtin, who had been informed of the assassination plot and of the counterplot to thwart it, called for silence. "I am deeply sorry to announce," he declared, "that Mr. Lincoln is suffering from a severe headache. While he would like to stay and meet everyone here, he regrets that he must retire to rest."

Curtin and the president-elect left the hall arm in arm, walking slowly toward the room that had been set aside for Lincoln's use, but when they reached a flight of stairs leading to a side entrance, they descended it as if they had suddenly decided that fresh air might make Lincoln feel better.

On the sidewalk they were met by Franciscus, who promptly threw a plaid shawl over Lincoln and then led the way to a waiting carriage. The president-elect was bareheaded—Pinkerton had requested that he leave his stovepipe hat behind—and the shawl covered his head and most of his body. As they entered the carriage, Curtin, as Allan had directed, told the driver to take them to the executive mansion, in case a spy was eavesdropping. However, as soon as they turned a corner, the horses were galloped to a railway siding at the lower end of town. Here, Franciscus had a locomotive with one car attached ready to roll, manned by a crack crew.

Accompanied by Ward Lamon, who was waiting for him, Lincoln climbed aboard the blacked-out special which immediately set off for Philadelphia. The engineer kept the throttle open as the train roared through the night, for he knew he had a clear stretch of track. Pinkerton had arranged that no other train was to use it from half-past five that afternoon until he gave permission to the chief dispatcher to resume routing traffic over it.

The Governor and Judd hastened to the hotel. They assured everyone that Lincoln was resting comfortably and that they were sure his headache was due only to fatigue. All evening Lincoln's friends continued to give the impression that he was still in Harrisburg. Although it was a difficult task to chat pleasantly with well-wishers and office-seekers while wondering if the counterplot would be successful, they accomplished it.

Even if they had not been able to keep up the pretense —and it did become known that Lincoln was no longer in the city—there was little chance for the Baltimore conspirators to learn the news in time to carry out the assassination. Pinkerton, who never left anything to chance, had arranged with Sanford that all telegrams from Harrisburg—except those sent to J. H. Hutchinson—flashed over the wires of the American Telegraph Company be held in the firm's Philadelphia office. In order to make sure there would be no mistake, one of the firm's officers took the place of the regular night operator.

While this arrangement prevented any information about Lincoln's flight being sent out over the wires controlled by Sanford, Pinkerton realized that the news could reach Philadelphia and then be relayed to Baltimore by means of the telegraph system of the Northern Central Railway. Although the master sleuth knew no one in authority in the office of this railroad, he was able to prevent its wires being used by the conspirators. Under his direction, an American Telegraph Company linesman climbed a pole outside the city limits and short-circuited them. Then, to make sure he had plugged this possible leak, the brash young man went to the Northern Central station and attempted to send a telegram, but was apologetically informed that the line was not working.

* * *

Meanwhile, Lincoln's train was rolling through the countryside at breakneck speed, stopping only to water the engine. When it pulled into West Philadelphia, Pinkerton and H. F. Kenney, an associate of Felton's, were waiting. The detective, Lamon and Lincoln climbed into a closed carriage which set out by a roundabout route for the station. Kenney, sitting with the driver, ordered him to draw up in the shadow of a high wall bordering the freight yard. As soon as the wheels stopped turning, the group dashed across the tracks and switches to a waiting train whose conductor was anxiously pacing up and down, glancing at his watch. He was due to pull out at ten minutes of eleven—it was almost time to leave—but he had been told to wait for a package from Felton which he was to deliver personally to one E. J. Allen—a favorite alias of Pinkerton's—at Willard's Hotel in Washington.

The fuming conductor had another worry. Evidently there was a very sick man traveling in the sleeping car. The stationmaster had told him that the invalid's sister had purchased the last three sections of the car so that her brother would not be disturbed by the other passengers. In addition to her solicitude for her "brother's" comfort, Kate Warne had also arranged that the rear roor of the car be kept open. This made it easy for Lincoln and La-mon to sneak aboard, as Felton had ordered that, when the train was "made up," the sleeping car be placed last in line.

Pretending he was a friend of the sick man who had of-fered to help care for him during the trip to Washington, Pinkerton impressed upon the conductor that "the poor chap mustn't be disturbed" and handed him a ticket. When Kenney saw Allan enter the car, he ran up the plat-form as if he had just arrived and handed Conductor Litz-enburg a package. Litzenburg grabbed it with one hand and signaled to the engineer with the other. Grumbling, the trainman stowed the package in a locker under one of the seats—he was taking no chance of losing his excuse for leaving five minutes behind schedule. Moreover, he was sure the thing was valuable, otherwise, why would Mr. Felton delay the train's departure for it? Fortunately, he was an honest man and made no attempt to peer inside the bundle. If he had, he would have been shocked. All it contained was old newspapers!

In the sleeping car, Pinkerton spoke briefly to Kate Warne and Bangs. Then the three checked their pistols. Allan left his assistants to guard Lincoln and, balancing himself against the sway of the train, made his way to the rear platform. Here he could watch for prearranged signals from his operatives, for, although everything had gone according to plan so far, Pinkerton was worried. A late report from Webster had informed him of the organization of regiments in many towns for the ostensible purpose of protecting railroad property, but which had actually been formed to destroy tracks and bridges if the South seceded.

Upon receipt of this news, Pinkerton had advised Felton to assign trusted employees to paint and repair all the line's bridges and also to secretly arm these men so that they could put up a defense in case of trouble. Tonight, in addition to Felton's crews, a Pinkerton operative stood guard at every switch, bridge and crossing. They had orders to signal with their bull's-eyes—two flashes, a short pause, then two more flashes—if all was well as Lincoln's train passed their post.

The bitter cold wind stung Pinkerton's eyes as he peered anxiously down the track, looking for the twinkling lights that blinked and vanished as quickly as a firefly's glow. When the train reached the Susquehanna River —where it was ferried from one bank to another—Allan became alarmed. Webster was on duty here and no lights could be seen. This could mean but one thing—danger ahead! Then, just when Pinkerton was about to force the engineer to hold the train, the reassuring flashes broke through the darkness.

Those signals continued to gleam all through the night. Operative after operative sent out the message "All's well —all's well," and the train rolled safely into the station in Baltimore at half-past three in the morning. Pinkerton was pleased to see that the station was deserted, but he could not relax. The most dangerous part of the trip was about to begin. Not only did the sleeping cars have to be hauled through the city from one station to another by horse, but there was also a two-hour layover until the train from Washington arrived from the West. The crosstown trip was uneventful, but the connecting train was late. Eventually it arrived, the sleeping car was hitched on and Pinkerton went back to his post on the rear platform, confident that the rest of the journey would go smoothly.

It did. Shortly after six, Lincoln left the car with Lamon and Allan. Immediately, a detachment of Pinkerton operatives closed in around them. While the station was crowded, at first no one recognized the president-elect, who remained well-wrapped in the shawl Franciscus had given him in Harrisburg, until he was almost out of the building. At that point, he was spotted by a congressman from Illinois, who rushed over to shake hands. Before the startled man knew what was happening, Pinkerton's crew surrounded him, while their employer hustled Lincoln outside.

General Scott and Seward were waiting in a carriage to take their chief to his hotel. As Lincoln joined them, Seward fervently exclaimed, "I never was so glad to see anyone in my life as I am to see you this morning!"

Pinkerton did not accompany Lincoln to Willard's. Nothing could happen to him now, and, besides, Allan had something important to do. He went back inside the station and sent a telegram to Harrisburg. It read: PLUMS ARRIVED WITH NUTS THIS MORNING.

Judd was jubilant when it arrived, for he knew that "Plums" was Pinkerton and "Nuts" was the code word for Lincoln—with no disrespect intended. He immediately informed the others concerned of the good news, then went to the door of a small room near the hotel's banquet hall and rapped three times in succession. This was followed by two well-spaced raps.

Inside, a keen-eyed man lowered the gun he had been pointing all night at the newspapermen who had been "covering" Lincoln's trip from Illinois to Washington. "Gentlemen," he announced, "I have something to tell you and then you are free to go. First, let me explain that I am a Pinkerton detective."

When the murmurs of surprise died down, the operative related the story of the assassination plot and summarized the arrangements that had enabled Lincoln to reach Washington safely. When he finished, the journalists rushed to the telegraph office to send their editors long stories describing how Pinkerton had outwitted the Baltimore conspirators.

Southern newspapers filled their columns with vehement denials that a plot against Lincoln ever existed. Anti-Lincoln papers in the North and some foreign publications, particularly the English comic weekly *Punch,* which was to ridicule everything Lincoln did during his administration—then make handsome amends upon his death—made fun of the entire incident. Cartoons with libelous captions, showing Lincoln wearing a plaid shawl and a deerstalker cap of the same material, were printed by the hundreds.

* * *

The morning after Lincoln reached Washington, Pinkerton was summoned to his suite. The president-elect graciously thanked him for his services.

After a few minutes of conversation, Allan left. He went directly to the station and took a train for Baltimore, where he held a conference with the operatives he had left in that city. They reported that most of the ringleaders in the assassination plot had fled to the South, fearing

that their names were known to the Federal authorities
and they would be arrested.

When he returned to Chicago, Pinkerton was beseiged
by journalists, asking for interviews. A great believer in
the value of publicity *after* a case was solved, Allan answered all their questions, characteristically stressing the
fact that he could have accomplished nothing without the
aid of his loyal operatives. Pinkerton singled Webster out
for special mention. "He among all the force who went
with me," the detective told the reporters, "deserves the
credit for saving the life of Mr. Lincoln, even more than
I do."

The journalists were delighted that Pinkerton talked so
freely, but, actually, the canny sleuth did not tell them
the whole story of his counterplot. He knew that they
would not think it funny—although he did—that the gun
which had kept their fellow newspapermen prisoners in
Harrisburg had not been loaded!

8

WE NEVER SLEEP

"Our Federal Union: it must be preserved."
—Jackson

FORT SUMTER FIRED UPON screamed newspaper head-
lines on April 13, 1861. Six days later, rioters stoned
a regiment of Massachusetts troops as it marched through
the streets of Baltimore. Within hours, telegraph lines and
railway bridges were destroyed, isolating Washington
from the North. Spontaneously, the flames of rebellion
flared throughout the slave-holding states and it would
take a long and bitter war before they would burn down
to ashes.

About a week after the Federal garrison under Major
Anderson withdrew from Sumter, a group of Chicago
businessmen and politicians asked Pinkerton to deliver
some important documents and letters to President Lincoln. It was seemingly impossible to reach the capital—
not only were the bridges down and railroad tracks torn
up, but every road was patrolled by armed bands of secessionists. Allan accepted the assignment and sent for Tim-

othy Webster. While he talked to his operative, Kate Warne sewed messages underneath Webster's coat collar and in the lining of his vest. When she was through, Webster set out for Washington.

His trip was without incident until he reached the Susquehanna River, where the train ferries had been burned by the rebels. However, the detective and his fellow passengers rowed to the other side. Here, they went to the local inn to spend the night. The innkeeper informed his guests that it was impossible to reach Baltimore from there except by walking and warned them that every traveler on the road was subjected to frequent and thorough examinations at numerous check points.

"What are we going to do, old man?" queried one of Webster's companions, who was obviously a well-educated young Englishman. "I must get to Washington as soon as possible and, if you'll pardon my intrusion upon your personal affairs, it seems as if you are also anxious to reach that city."

"We won't have to walk," Webster replied confidently. "I'm sure this fifty-dollar bill will convince some farmer to hitch up and give us a ride in his wagon to Baltimore."

He was right. Sleeping fretfully in the jolting wagon, awakened often by sentries and ordered to state their business, they finally arrived in Perryman. The soldiers on duty here were members of Webster's old regiment and they hailed their former comrade with shouts of welcome and friendly jeers. At the local military headquarters, the detective was warmly greeted by the officer in charge who, upon request, instantly provided a pass permitting the pair to travel to Washington.

Impressed by Webster's friendship with the military and the ease with which he had secured the pass, the Englishman became convinced that the detective was an

important official in the Confederate Government. Therefore, he confided that he was a courier, carrying papers
of value to the Southern cause to the British consul in
the capital, and expressed fear that they would not be
delivered.

"We'll get them to Washington," Webster promised, but
silently determined that the documents would be delivered to the Federal authorities, not to the British consul.
He tried hard to evolve some scheme by which he could
get possession of them. He could think of nothing and
was about to resort to force, when they stopped at an inn
for lunch. Just as Webster dismounted, he saw a friend
of his who was a staunch supporter of the Union. Under
the pretext of asking the groom to water and curry the
horses, the detective managed to tell his friend who his
companion was, and asked him to arrange for his capture.

After lunch, the two resumed their journey and soon
reached the outskirts of Washington. Suddenly, a group
of soldiers appeared, surrounded the wagon, accused its
occupants of being spies and hauled them off to the
guardhouse. Unknown to the Englishman, Webster was
freed immediately. On a borrowed horse, he rode swiftly
to the capital, went directly to the White House and,
upon being ushered into Nicolay's office, took off his coat,
tore off the collar, slit the lining of his vest and removed
the messages he had brought from Chicago.

Early the next morning, Webster was called to the
White House where, after wryly commenting, "I hear you
are hard on clothes, Mr. Webster," Abraham Lincoln expressed his appreciation of the detective's services. The
president also revealed that the documents taken from the
courier contained the names of a great number of Southern sympathizers in Washington. He then informed Webster that he had two important telegrams that he wished

to send, but was unable to do so because the rebels had
cut the telegraph wires linking Washington with the rest
of the nation. "Would you please take them and send them
for me?" he asked. "One is to Major-General George B.
McClellan in Ohio, the other is to a person I believe you
know, Allan Pinkerton of Chicago."

Webster willingly accepted the telegrams, placed them
in a hollow cane and set out for Chicago by way of Pittsburgh. At the first Federal outpost he reached that had
telegraphic equipment, he asked the commanding officer
to dispatch the presidential messages and then continued
his journey.

*   *   *

President Lincoln's wire to Pinkerton asked him to come
to Washington as soon as possible. Delaying only long
enough to telegraph Webster to remain in Pittsburgh until further notice, Allan started for the capital. After a
roundabout trip—across Chesapeake Bay to Annapolis,
Maryland, by boat and then on to Washington by rail—he
finally reached his destination. Lincoln greeted Allan
warmly and then conducted him to a special meeting of
the Cabinet, so that the detective might suggest something he felt would prove of benefit to his country. He
wanted to "discuss a secret service department in hopes
of ascertaining the social, political and patriotic relations
of the numerous suspected people in and about Washington."

Such an agency was sorely needed, for the War, Navy
and Justice Departments were not organized to investigate traitors or gather military information. Even though
such loyal and brave men as Nathan Hale had served the
nation as spies, there was a general feeling that espionage
was un-American. As a result, while Pinkerton assured the

president and his advisors that Washington was teeming with Confederate agents and Southern sympathizers and made clear the value of learning the South's military plans before they were put into action, his suggestions for a secret service met with a cool reception.

Finally, Lincoln brought the meeting to a close by saying, "You'll hear from us in a few days."

A week passed, but no word came from the White House. In disgust, Pinkerton went to Philadelphia, where he found a letter waiting for him. It was from his old friend George McClellan, formerly of the Illinois Central Railroad. After informing Allan that he would like to see him in Cincinnati as soon as possible, McClellan wrote, "If you telegraph me, better use your first name alone. Let no one know you come to see me, and keep quiet as possible."

This was mysterious enough to satisfy even Allan Pinkerton. He telegraphed McClellan, then took the train for Pittsburgh, where he planned to meet Webster and accompany him to Ohio. Unable to locate his operative at his hotel, Allan went for a walk and found his assistant, back against a wall, gun in hand, defending himself against a mob that was threatening to lynch him as a Confederate spy.

As Pinkerton pushed his way through the throng, he drew his own gun and, when he reached Webster's side, yelled, "Stop! Stop! I know this man! He is not a spy. I'll kill the first person that takes another step forward!"

Cowed by the two guns, the crowd fell back. After its ringleaders held a whispered conference, one of them suggested, "Very well, if he isn't a spy, let's go to the mayor's office and prove it."

Pinkerton agreed and everyone set out for City Hall.

On the way, they met the chief of police, who recognized Allan, and the would-be lynchers dispersed.

In Cincinnati, Pinkerton "soon found that my services were needed, and putting aside all considerations of private or business nature, I yielded a ready and cheerful response to the call, and during my connection with what was afterwards known as the secret service of the government, I rendered every assistance that lay in my power to further the cause of union, and to serve the country of my adoption."

McClellan, unlike Lincoln's official family, was convinced of the need for a secret service agency, and he had no trouble persuading Pinkerton, who was weary of waiting to hear from Washington, to organize one for his command. Allan established a headquarters and telegraphed for his best operatives. They reported, as directed, to Major E. J. Allen. Pinkerton used this alias all during the war, and many of his military associates thought it was his real name. Upon meeting him years later, they still would mistakenly address him as Major Allen.

As a spy—both Federal and Confederate military authorities preferred to call their secret agents "scouts"—the major seldom wore a uniform. He soon discovered, as did the members of the Signal Bureau of the Confederate Army, the South's espionage unit, that valuable information could often be secured without difficulty. Sometimes all a spy had to do was read newspapers and magazines. For example, *Harper's Weekly* published a well-illustrated description of the *Monitor* long before that vessel sailed from New York to meet the *Merrimac* in the battle that changed the course of naval history. Moreover, full details of how, when and where generals planned to engage the enemy were often known to newspaper readers in the North before troops in the field received their orders.

Therefore, Lee assigned scouts to smuggle Union newspapers through the lines and, after reading them, frequently revised his strategy.

Reporters and the artists who did the sketches from which newspaper and magazine illustrations were made had little trouble securing either news or pictures. People on both sides talked openly about troop movements, shipments of material and what their sons and husbands had written in uncensored letters from camp and battlefield. Officers in charge of military installations gladly escorted strangers through them and willingly answered questions. In fact, Theodore Davis, an artist for *Harper's,* toured the South with William H. Russell, war correspondent for the London *Times,* and although Davis frankly admitted his connection with the Northern publication, he was permitted to inspect fortifications.

Davis had no trouble until he reached Memphis, Tennessee, where, as his editor reported to the subscribers of *Harper's* ". . . a Vigilance Committee inquired after the fashion of these bodies, who he was, where he came from, what he was doing, where he was going, and whether he didn't need any hanging. Having obtained answers to these various queries, the Committee then proceeded to inspect Mr. Davis' trunk, which they overhauled with commendable thoroughness. Finding at the bottom of the trunk a number of sketches made for us, they examined them minutely, and each member, by way of remembering Mr. Davis, pocketed two or three of the most striking."

The account of Davis' encounter with the vigilantes was well-illustrated as the artist had boldly drawn several sketches of the search of his trunk while it was taking place. The Committeemen were so delighted at the prospect of having their pictures in *Harper's* they did not confiscate them!

Pinkerton also had an unusual adventure in Memphis. Although Allan had sent Webster and several other operatives to gather information in Kentucky and Tennessee, McClellan requested the detective to investigate conditions there himself. Pinkerton first went to Kentucky. Here he listened to many and talked to a few. He reported to his superior that, in his opinion, Kentucky would stay out of the war for a while, as some of its citizens supported secession, while others favored the Union. Eventually, however, the state would side with the North. His prediction proved correct when the legislature of Kentucky passed a law proclaiming the state's strict neutrality, then, shortly afterwards, repealed it, whereupon the state took up arms to defend the Union.

Because train service was irregular, Pinkerton bought a horse in Bowling Green, Kentucky, and rode to Tennessee. In Nashville, he learned much of value, then went on to Memphis. Posing as a Georgian, he walked openly about the city, making friends with everyone he met. However, during one of his strolls he saw a slave auction for the first time and became so enraged that he almost gave himself away. Fortunately, he recovered his composure and continued to play his part so well, that General Pillow of the Confederate Army invited him to dine. As the two talked over their after-dinner cigars, Pillow disclosed military secrets with the same frankness as had the innocent Negroes working on the breastworks being thrown up to defend Memphis in case of a Union attack.

Confident that his masquerade was succeeding, Pinkerton gave no thought to the possibility of being unmasked as a spy. Then, one morning, while shaving, a Negro boy, employed by the hotel, burst into his room crying, "Massa, you're a dead man if you don't get out of here. They're going to shoot you for being a spy. Go down the back stairs—I got your horse there!"

As Pinkerton hastily wiped the lather from his face and threw on his coat, the boy told him that he had been recognized by a Confederate officer who had formerly lived in Chicago. Tossing a handful of coins to Jem, Allan dashed down the stairs, sprang to the saddle and fled. Eventually, he reached the Union lines and relayed the information he had gathered to McClellan.

A few days later, while Major Allen was spying in Mississippi, he had another close escape. In Jackson, he rose at five—as he usually did—and walked about noting military preparations, then went to a barbershop for a shave.

As he sat down, the barber asked, with a thick German accent, "Ain't you Mr. Pingerdon?"

"What are you talking about! Certainly not!"

"Dot's funny. You look like da Mr. Pingerdon I shaved ven I vorked in da barvershop in da Sherman Hotel in Shecago."

"Never mind who I look like. Shave me and let me out of here!"

Muttering to himself, the barber set to work. As soon as he was finished, Pinkerton did get out of there as fast as possible and returned to Cincinnati.

Meanwhile, two Pinkerton operatives, disguised as an English lord and his servant, were traveling through the western part of Virginia. Allan had reason to believe that Northern sympathizers there wanted to break away from the rest of the state—which they did in 1863, when West Virginia entered the Union. He wished to learn if they would help McClellan, who was planning an invasion of the region. Pyrce Lewis, the operative who was pretending to be a member of British nobility, was English by birth. He looked like a lord and his disguise was excellent.

Dressed in well-tailored suits, wearing a high silk hat, with Pinkerton's diamond ring on his finger, Lewis, armed with forged letters of introduction from prominent Englishmen, rode through the countryside in a fine carriage drawn by a matched pair wearing silver-studded harness. Beside Lewis on the carriage seat were cases of champagne. This he shared freely, along with the contents of his cigar case, which was embossed with an ivory British lion. All this, plus his servant's humble "Certainly, m'Lord," convinced everyone, from farmers to field officers, that Pyrce Lewis was what he pretended to be.

Actually, Pyrce and his companion were extremely lucky, as they were terribly careless, often telling conflicting stories to the same people. Nevertheless, they not only found out that McClellan would meet little resistance from civilians when he invaded, they also collected a mass of vital information. This was due in no small part to Pyrce's excellent acting. Stopped once by a cavalry troop and asked for a pass, "m'Lord" apologetically explained that he didn't think a visitor from overseas needed one. The soldiers let him through with the polite suggestion that he visit headquarters and ask for one from Colonel George D. Patton—whose grandson was to achieve fame as a tank commander in World War II. Patton proved to be most gracious and invited Lewis to tour the local fortifications.

The secret service agent, sensing something suspicious in the Colonel's eagerness to show him about, declined, saying, "No, if you don't mind. I saw so many forts in the Crimea. However, I would appreciate a pass so that I can continue my travels."

He received it, and the carriage, with the British army trunk strapped on behind, rolled into Charleston, Virginia. Here, Lewis charmed General Wise and his staff with tales of battles in the Crimea—which he had never seen, but had read about before leaving Cincinnati. His Lordship's knowledge of the British rationing system— also learned from books—deeply impressed his hosts, who informed him that the Charleston commissary issued 3,500 rations a day, thus telling Lewis the number of men stationed there.

When the two operatives returned to Cincinnati, Pinkerton was waiting for them. After listening to their report and reading their notes, he sent McClellan a long telegram. Upon receiving it, McClellan ordered Lewis to Union headquarters on the Kanawha River, to give General Cox all the military information he had gathered.

Cox listened to Lewis, but refused to believe the agent's facts and figures, claiming that he had far more accurate data. In common with many military men, Cox had little respect for advice from civilians on how to conduct a campaign. However, his staff sided with Lewis, and the General reluctantly gave the order to attack Charleston, which was captured by his troops.

Unlike Cox, McClellan did not hesitate to take full advantage of the information Pinkerton's men had gathered in Virginia. He launched his invasion, winning one skirmish after another. Relatively unimportant as these were, they encouraged the North, which had been suffering a succession of defeats on the battlefield. As a result, President Lincoln, who had been desperately seeking a general capable of leading the Union to victory, appointed McClellan commander-in-chief.

When "Little Mac" left for Washington to assume his new post, he was accompanied by the man responsible for his promotion—Major E. J. Allen.

9

"Some people are very resourceful."
—Nash

McCLELLAN'S PROMOTION raised the hopes of the North. For the first time since the outbreak of the war, when the bells in Boston rang day and night to announce three thousand men had answered Lincoln's call to arms and a Wisconsin judge and jury left the courtroom to enlist, expectation of an early victory spread through the loyal states. To be sure, some military men did not approve of "Little Mac," but most newspapers did. One reported: "General McClellan, whose able management of the campaign in West Virginia is worthy of all praise, has been called to Washington to take command of the Army of the Potomac."

When McClellan and Pinkerton arrived in the capital, they found the city in a turmoil. Southern sympathizers were openly laughing at the Union soldiers who had panicked at Bull Run, dropped their guns, thrown away their equipment and fled the battlefield. Secessionist sneers

were bad enough, but the authorities were more concerned with discovering how Beauregard, commander of
the Confederate forces, knew where and when the Union
troops would attack. It was obvious that Washington was
filled with spies. The question was, who were they?

Despite the fact that McClellan wanted Major Allen to
do undercover work behind enemy lines, President Lincoln's secretary of war, Simon Cameron, who was to be
removed from office for inefficiency and replaced by Ed-
win Stanton, asked him to disclose "traitorous organizations." Pinkerton took over a building on I Street in Washington and used it as his headquarters while organizing
the first government-authorized secret service agency in
American history.

Meanwhile, Webster and other operatives continued
their spying in Southern states, sending back a constant
stream of reports. Sometimes these daring agents gained
vital information with absolutely no risk to themselves.
The operatives assigned to discover the destinations of the
troop trains leaving Richmond had only to copy the names
of the regiments that were being shipped to the front
from a blackboard that hung in the station! On the
other hand, Pinkerton's staff often faced death from a
sniper's bullet when slipping by Confederate outposts,
and they were in constant danger of being lynched by
Vigilante Committees if their true identities were discovered. Years later, Pinkerton was to write, "Shrewd and
daring operatives, men and women, trained for the work,
moved in and out among the rebel troops at all times and
places."

Actually, despite this statement, there were no trained
espionage agents on Major Allen's staff. Nevertheless, his
assistants performed remarkably well considering the fact
that they had no preparation for their tasks. However, the

roster of the secret service included operatives with
unique specialties that more than made up for their lack
of training. Among them was Dave Graham, originally a
member of the 21st New York Infantry, who used to en-
tertain his comrades in arms by pretending to be unable
to speak without stuttering. Major Pinkerton happened to
overhear one of his performances—an example of the famous Pinkerton luck—and when it was over, had a long
talk with Private Graham. During their conversation, the
Major learned that Graham could also act as if he were
stupid and had the ability to imitate an epileptic. Shortly
afterwards, the infantry lost "Stuttering Dave," but the
secret service gained a most valuable agent.

Disguised as a foolish pack-peddler who stuttered, Graham visited Confederate installations, selling small articles and recording large amounts of military information.
Once he was almost forced to join the Confederate Army
but escaped service by falling into a "fit" just as he was
being sworn in by the recruiting officer.

Pinkerton took every advantage of the various skills of
the female operatives on the Agency staff all through the
war. In Washington, Mrs. Warne made friends of many
women who supported the South. From them, she gained
much information, thus substantiating the claim she had
made when applying for the job that made her the first
woman detective in America; "that she could go and worm
out secrets in many places to which it was impossible for
male detectives to gain access." While Kate Warne did
not go behind enemy lines, Mrs. E. H. Baker did. Thanks
to her, the success of the Federal blockade that slowly
starved the South into submission was assured.

Even during the early days of the war, the blockade was
causing hardship in the South—although it was making
millionaires out of a few reckless men. Baltimore mer-

chants with stores in Richmond, Virginia, outfitted fast boats to run the blockade, frequently making $50,000 profit on a single cargo. Richmond residents always knew when one of these vessels arrived. Advertisements would appear in the newspapers stating, "New Goods by steamer this day." However, most of the cargoes consisted of expensive articles, and the poorer people felt the pangs of hunger. Then, suddenly, rumors began to circulate in Washington that caused those in charge of the blockade grave concern. Before long, it was an open secret that all the ships that patrolled the mouth of the James River would soon be sunk—the Confederates, according to hearsay, were building a submarine capable of destroying the entire Union fleet.

When this report reached Major Allen's office, he sent for Mrs. Baker, one of his female operatives, who had formerly lived in Richmond. She was instructed to write a letter to friends in that city saying that she wanted to return. Because there was no regular mail service between northern and southern points, the letter was given to a member of the "underground express"—men who clandestinely carried messages and small packages from Washington to Richmond for a large fee.

"The battery is supposedly being constructed at the Tredegar Iron Works," Pinkerton informed Mrs. Baker. "Your job is to find out if such a device does exist and if it does, learn all about it."

There was no doubt in Pinkerton's mind that the Confederates were building a submarine—John Holland, an American inventor, had proved such underwater vessels practical in 1808—to destroy the ships blockading their shores. The detective also knew that no other industrial plant in the South was as well-equipped for the task as the Tredegar Works. A world-famous concern, Tredegar had manufactured locomotives for European and American railroads and had furnished anchors and anchor chains to the United States Navy for years. With the outbreak of the war, the works, drawing on its own iron mines, had become one of the South's largest munitions factories. It was so heavily guarded that a regiment of soldiers would find storming its gates impossible, but Mrs. Baker was sure she could carry out her mission.

Pinkerton provided his agent with a pass that permitted her to go through Union lines, and, after a long and roundabout journey, Mrs. Baker arrived at the capital of the Confederacy's most war-minded state, where she was greeted by her old friends, Captain and Mrs. Atwater. The Atwaters were socially prominent and introduced Mrs. Baker to many army officers. These gentlemen gallantly invited her to military drills, to ride along the breastworks or to visit fortifications, little knowing that their charming companion made careful notes of everything she saw.

One afternoon, Captain Atwater, himself, escorted her and several other ladies to "see a new weapon that will break the blockade." Peering through a pair of binoculars belonging to her host, Mrs. Baker saw a submarine manned by a crew dressed in divers' suits, who obtained air from long tubes attached to a green float above their vessel. The crew, Atwater explained, drew close to their target, attached explosives and then pulled away, after lighting a long fuse to ignite the gunpowder. "This is just a model," he told the sight-seers. "We are going to test it on that scow moored in the middle of the river."

As he spoke, the scow blew to bits. No one cheered louder than Mrs. Baker, and her enthusiasm prompted Atwater to take her to the Tredegar plant several days later to see the full-sized submarine being constructed. As soon as she returned home, Mrs. Baker made a sketch of the

underwater boat and carefully hid it. Her greatest problem was to place it in Pinkerton's hands. Therefore, in
about a week she began complaining of feeling restless
and told the Atwaters that she wished to return to Chicago. The Captain procured a pass that enabled her to
leave Richmond and go to Washington on the flag-of-truce
boat which plied regularly between the two cities.

Pinkerton was waiting when she arrived. Always a gentleman, he tipped his hat as Mrs. Baker approached. His
operative promptly took off her bonnet in response! She
ripped it apart and removed her notes and the sketches
she had made of the submarine. Her chief wasted no time
in passing these on to Gideon Wells, the secretary of the
navy, with the suggestion that he "order the look-outs to
watch for a water-colored surface float and when it is
sighted, drag for the air tubes. This will mean the end of
the crew. Then the submarine can be destroyed."

Wells took this advice, and the South's hopes of raising
the blockade sank to the bottom of the sea.

While his operatives were busy spying in enemy territory, Pinkerton was not idle. He was never to perform
such spectacular feats as some of his agents—one actually
boldly walked into the headquarters of the Confederate
secret service in Richmond and learned how it operated—
but he worked day and night for the Union cause. When
Stanton assumed the post of secretary of war, he directed
Pinkerton to do everything in his power to eliminate treasonable activities in Washington. Long hampered in his
investigations of suspected spies by the capital's police
force, which numbered many secessionists among its
members, the detective immediately devoted a great deal
of his time to reorganizing the force, with the help of
Colonel Andrew Porter, provost-marshal for Washington.

Despite his many duties in the capital, Pinkerton did

manage to get away once in a while for scouting trips. His mission on all of these forays was to determine the strength of the forces facing McClellan. Unfortunately, while the Major could sift rumor from fact, investigate and trap suspected traitors and break down codes that revealed the identity of Confederate spies holding Federal office, he usually miscalculated when estimating the size of enemy troop concentrations. One historian caustically wrote that Pinkerton "could not tell a battalion from a regiment and the sunshine glancing on the fixed bayonets of a brigade made it look like a division."

When not in the field, Major Allen was at his desk in secret service headquarters on I Street. Here, he read reports from his agents—he insisted on seeing them personally—or talked to operatives, in the hope of learning some significant fact they had neglected to put down in writing. In addition, he interviewed those who had slipped through Confederate picket lines and surrendered to Union soldiers, if his assistants, after screening them, thought their stories would interest their superior. The staff also had orders to send along any runaway slaves who were willing to return South and engage in espionage, in order that he might determine by talking with them whether they were capable of secret service work. Major Allen gratefully recognized one such runaway, Jem, the young Negro who had saved his life in Memphis. The boy was assigned to several missions and proved an outstanding spy.

However, no Negro was as valuable to the secret service as was John Scobell. While interviewing him, Major Allen was deeply impressed with his intelligence and with the clarity with which he described all that he had seen since leaving Richmond. Scobell was ordered to Leonardtown, Maryland, to work with Webster, who was now acting

President Lincoln holds a conference at the battlefront with General McClellan and Allan Pinkerton ("Major Allen").

Allan Pinkerton in 1867.

Allan Pinkerton and his wife Joan, from an old daguerreotype.

Major Allen (Allan Pinkerton) returns from scouting enemy positions for General McClellan during the Civil War.

William A. Pinkerton when he served as a teen-age spy for the Union Secret Service in 1863, and, in 1921, when he was an effective member of Pinkerton's National Detective Agency, founded by his father.

Secret Service Field Headquarters of the Army of the Potomac encamped before Antietam.

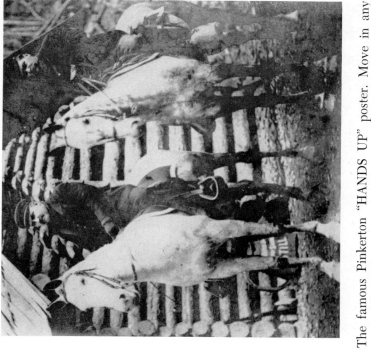

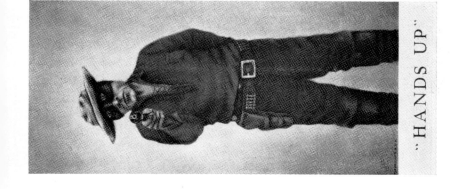

"HANDS UP"

(*Left*) The famous Pinkerton "HANDS UP" poster. Move in any direction and the masked man seems to be aiming at your eyes!
(*Right*) Robert A. Pinkerton and William A. Pinkerton on the trail of outlaws in the West.

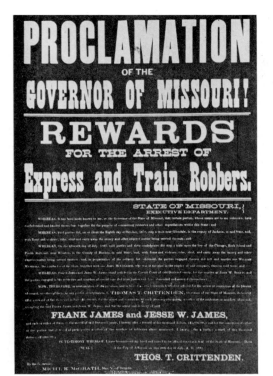

(*Left*) The State of Missouri offers a reward for the arrest of the James Boys. (*Below*) Revolver used by William A. Pinkerton in pursuing bank and train robbers on the western frontier.

A pair of desperados who were out to get the Pinkerton operatives—Frank and Jesse James.

Although "The Wild Bunch" thought it amusing to have their picture taken wearing "store clothes," the photograph led to their capture.

ROBBERS KILLED
  Clell Miller
  Bill Stiles, alias
    Chadwell
  Charlie Pitts
WOUNDED & CAPTURED
  Cole Younger
  Jim Younger
  Bob Younger
ESCAPED
  Jesse James
  Frank James

Artist's drawing of the unsuccessful raid on the First National Bank of Northfield, Minnesota, by the James and Younger Brothers' Gang, on September 7, 1876. Only the James Brothers escaped.

Timothy Webster, "The Spy of the Rebellion."

William A. Pinkerton (center), with Pat Connell, Special Agent for the
Southern Express Company, and Sam Finley, Assistant Special Agent
for the Company, prepared for action—and they had plenty of it!

The origin of the "Rogues Gallery"–reproduction of a Pinkerton identification file card, showing a photograph of Charles Ross, train robber, on one side and giving his record and description on the reverse side.

PINKERTON'S NATIONAL DETECTIVE AGENCY, INC.

NAME ADEARISHE   55-0-788   FOALED 3/7/52   COLOR Ches   SEX Colt

SIRE *Shifting Sands 2nd   DAM Miss Hurricane   BREEDER Miss Dorothy Palmer
MARKINGS TAKEN: DATE 3/5/55   AT Hialeah Y   BY M.J.Reilly
PHOTOGRAPHED: DATE "   AT "   BY P.Downick
OWNER Mt. Vernon Stable   TRAINER L.Phillips

FOAL CERTIFICATE VERIFICATION	
Certificate No. 522468	
Tattoo No. H2468	
Tattoo No. X	(Verified)
Certificate Examined	X
Certificate Marks Complete	X
Markings Agree	X
Basic Check Satisfactory	X
Identifier MJR	
Date 3 / 5 / 55	

HEAD Irregular star connected stripe to between bridge of nose. Snip between nostrils nearer left nostril. Cowlick between bottom of eyes.

LEFT FORE LEG /

LEFT HIND LEG /

RIGHT HIND LEG /

RIGHT FORE LEG /

BODY Cowlick right side and left side of neck near mane.

SUBSEQUENT SCARS
CHARACTERISTICS
WITHERS   RUMP

REMARKS

Another type of identification perfected by Pinkerton's National Detective Agency, Inc. A photograph and complete description of every race horse in America is kept on file.

Two men wanted—and found—by the Pinkertons, Maximillian Schoenbein, alias Max Shinburne, alias Baron Schindle, celebrated bank vault and safe burglar (*left*) and Jack Phillips, alias "Junka," burglar, in an "unwilling" pose!

Like his famous grandfather, Allan Pinkerton, who served as a Major in the Intelligence Corps during World War I, refused to remain safely behind the combat lines. He was severely gassed while up forward.

Robert A. Pinkerton, great-grandson of the original founder, now heads Pinkerton's National Detective Agency.

as a double agent, giving the Confederacy true but trivial information supplied by the War Department while gathering vital data for the North. The two successfully carried out several difficult assignments.

Usually they worked without orders. When Webster's landlord introduced him to a former Union Army doctor who had deserted and was carrying documents to Judah P. Benjamin, Secretary of War for the Confederacy, the operative arranged for Scobell to get a close look at the deserter. Then, as the doctor took a stroll that evening, Scobell knocked him down, stole the documents and gave them to Webster who said, "Good work, John! Now do you want to take them to Washington?"

"I don't think that will be necessary, sir," replied Scobell. "Meet me behind your hotel about half-past eleven tonight."

Scobel took Webster to a house in the Negro section of Leonardtown, knocked on the door and then whispered, "Friends of Uncle Abe." The door swung open to reveal a meeting of the Loyal League, a secret organization composed of slaves. Webster was asked to deliver a short talk and he did so. When the meeting broke up, the president of the group offered to take the stolen documents to the secret service's headquarters in Washington. They were on Major Allen's desk within a few days.

Besides working with Webster, Scobell also acted as the dull-witted servant of Mrs. Carrie Lawton, who, like her husband, was a Pinkerton operative in Richmond. On other occasions he worked alone. Scobell's beautiful baritone voice made him a welcome visitor at Confederate campfires. As he sang, Scobell kept his ears open far wider than his mouth and sent back facts and figures of great value to the Union cause.

Strangely, Scobell spoke with a pronounced Scotch ac-

cent because he had had a Scot for a master. His singing
of "Annie Laurie" pleased the Scotch captain of a Rappa-
hannock River packet boat so much that he offered the
secret agent a job as a deck hand. Scobell accepted and
the voyage carried him deep into enemy territory. Eventually, he jumped ship, returned overland to Washington
and gave Major Allen a lengthy report on everything he
had seen and heard.

In employing runaway slaves as spies, Pinkerton was
taking advantage of General Benjamin Butler's device to
bypass the Fugitive Slave Law. This act—part of the Compromise of 1850 which Henry Clay had hoped would settle the differences between North and South—stated that
runaway slaves were to be returned to their masters. Because of the war, this ruling created a problem. If the
Negroes belonged to owners loyal to the Union, they
should, by law, be held for the duration of the conflict and
then given back. On the other hand, no one knew what
should be done with runaway slaves belonging to the
secessionists. General Butler neatly solved the puzzle by
applying the word "contraband" to all fugitive slaves—a
term used to designate military property in transit on the
high seas—and employed them as laborers, cooks and
hospital attendants.

Major Allen also gave scouting and other assignments
to a bright young man, not quite sixteen years old, who
had left school to join the secret service. Alert, quick-wit-
ted and very observant, this most capable agent was listed
on the roster as William Allan Pinkerton. In time, William
was to become almost as famous a detective as his father
and win the fear and respect of lawbreakers all over the
world.

❖   ❖   ❖

It did not take Major Allen very long to discover that "secret traitorous organizations" were not hampered by his establishment of martial law in Washington. The South, he informed the authorities, knew the position "of every regiment and brigade and the contemplated movements of the commanders and the time of the proposed action." There was, he continued, no doubt of the efficiency of Confederate espionage in Washington.

While routine investigations unmasked some spies who were masquerading as loyal citizens of the North, most of those arrested were unimportant members of the enemy's far-reaching espionage network. As a general rule, such individuals were released after taking an oath of allegiance to the Federal Government. Meanwhile, military secrets continued to reach the South with the same regularity with which Union and Confederate pickets exchanged newspapers and swapped tobacco for food. Major Allen's job was to find out who was sending this confidential material to Richmond and how they were securing it.

For a time, this seemed an impossible task. Then, shortly after Bull Run, Thomas A. Scott, assistant secretary of war, visited secret service headquarters. In passing, he suggested that it might be well for Major Allen's organization to "watch a lady whose moves had excited suspicion." Scott could have spoken far more bluntly. The lady in question had not only secured copies of his notes written during a council with high-ranking military leaders, but she had placed them in the hands of the Confederate commander in Richmond the day after the meeting was held!

10

"Everything that deceives may be said to enchant."
—Plato

THE LADY WHO HAD "excited suspicion," according to Scott, was Rose Greenhow, an attractive widow whose residence on Sixteenth Street, near the White House, was the gathering place of Washington society. Mrs. Greenhow had not always lived in such fashionable surroundings or been on intimate terms with important people. As a girl, she had left her parents' farm and gone to Washington to assist her aunt, who ran the Congressional Boarding House in the Old Capitol Building. One of the tenants was John Calhoun, the outspoken champion of the slave-holding states in the Senate. He taught the impressionable teen-ager to respect learning and inspired her with a desire to serve the South.

Other boarders—particularly the younger ones—paid Rose, who was a most attractive girl, a great deal of attention, but she eventually married Robert Greenhow. Her husband was an extremely well-educated man who was editor of a newspaper that supported slavery and the doctrine of States' Rights. This was the belief that prevailed in the South, that the Federal Government was merely the agent of the states and that, therefore, an individual's first allegiance was to his state rather than to the Union. It was this view that prompted Robert E. Lee to decline the command of the United States Army, offered to him by President Lincoln when the War Between the States began and to lead troops from his native state, Virginia, for the Confederacy instead.

When the Greenhows set up housekeeping, John Calhoun left the Congressional Boarding House and came to live with them. Although Calhoun was an extremely important man, the fact that the "Great Nullifier" was their house guest did not make the Greenhows socially acceptable. However, when Mrs. Greenhow's niece married Senator Stephen A. Douglas, the unsuccessful Democratic candidate for the presidency in the election of 1860, and her sister became the wife of the nephew of Dolly Madison, the attractive widow of the fourth president of the United States, practically everyone who had previously snubbed the Greenhows frantically tried to become on intimate terms with them. Nevertheless, Rose Greenhow was not active socially until after her husband's death. Then, almost overnight, she became the most talked about hostess in Washington.

There was a very good reason for this—the prestige value of the guest lists for her parties. One such roster included, among others: President James Buchanan; William H. Seward, who was to be Lincoln's secretary of state and later would expand the territorial limits of the United States by purchasing Alaska from Russia; Jefferson Davis, future president of the Confederacy; and Senator Henry Wilson, who became vice-president in Grant's sec-

ond administration. Lesser-known figures were also frequent visitors at the Greenhow mansion—to the delight of
neighborhood gossips—but they never attended the formal
functions. They were, for the most part, young army officers and minor officials in various governmental departments who found it most pleasant and very relaxing to
chat about their work as the charming widow served them
tea and cake.

As a result of her friendship with everyone from members of the Cabinet to holders of petty posts, Rose Greenhow was not only an influential woman, she was also
exceedingly well-informed about proposed governmental
policies and the personal plans of politicians. Moreover,
she had never forgotten any of the teachings of John Calhoun and constantly expressed to her confidants the wish
that she might find some way to use her position and
knowledge to aid the cause of the South.

Her first opportunity to do so came shortly after Abraham Lincoln's election. Thomas Jordan, a Virginian, serving as a lieutenant in the United States Army, had a long
talk with Mrs. Greenhow previous to resigning his commission and returning home. When Jordan left the house
on Sixteenth Street, he had Mrs. Greenhow's solemn promise to use her power and position in Washington as a spy
for the South, in the event that the Union was dissolved.
She had a copy of a complicated cipher to use in trans-
mitting information to secessionist headquarters in Richmond.

No spy ever worked with more enthusiasm than Mrs.
Greenhow. When the War Between the States finally
broke out she was ready, having set up a tightly knit
espionage unit that functioned remarkably well. After
Bull Run—she had sent the Confederacy all the details of
the North's battle plans by a young woman courier who

carried the message in her hair—Beauregard wrote a letter
to Mrs. Greenhow, expressing his appreciation "for the
most accurate information." It certainly was accurate.
Federal authorities, stunned and puzzled by the unexplained leakage of vital military secret data, frankly admitted that the facts and figures used to defeat the North
could be found only in locked and well-guarded files in
the War Department. No wonder Jefferson Davis sent
Mrs. Greenhow a personal letter by a scout which ended
with, "The Confederacy owes you a debt."

Despite the war and Mrs. Greenhow's open and well-
known support of the South, important government officials still continued to call at her house. Moreover, she
was always included in the gay groups invited to hold
picnics in military installations or to attend a review of
the troops guarding Washington. The lengthy reports she
made after taking part in one of these social affairs and
sent secretly to Richmond were usually accompanied by
blueprints that had mysteriously vanished from the offices
of generals or admirals in the War and Navy Departments.
Her spy ring extended everywhere. No matter what plans
were being prepared or what decision was reached in a
secret conference between statesmen and military leaders, Mrs. Greenhow soon knew all the facts. Although
barred from the Old Capitol Prison—formerly her aunt's
Congressional Boarding House where she had worked as
a girl—because the superintendent noticed that the names
of his charges were known in Richmond the day after
Mrs. Greenhow brought reading and writing materials to
them, this clever woman still had no difficulty in learning who had been arrested.

*   *   *

After General Scott's visit to his headquarters, Major Allen quietly began to learn all he could about the charming, wealthy and prominent Mrs. Rose Greenhow. Suspicious by nature, unswerving in his loyalty to the Union, unawed by the lady's social prestige and political connections, the head of the secret service kept Mrs. Greenhow under constant surveillance. As was to be expected, she was well aware that she was being watched, but, confident that her powerful friends would protect her, she laughed at the possibility that she might be arrested and continued to send information to Richmond.

However, clever as she was, Mrs. Greenhow did not realize one vital fact. No man could be more determined and persevering than Allan Pinkerton when working on a case, especially when it was in behalf of his country. He was absolutely convinced that, if a detective of "strict integrity and honorable conduct" stayed on a job long enough, he would gather the evidence necessary to convict a criminal. He once summed up his feelings in this regard in the preface to one of his books: "Vice may triumph for a time, crime may flaunt its victories in the face of honest toilers, but in the end the law will follow the wrong-doer to a bitter fate, and dishonor and punishment will be the portion of those who sin."

Major Allen also had something to say about crime—especially the crime of treason. In November, 1861, he sent a formal note to the War Department, expressing his opinions of Mrs. Greenhow. He called the attention of his superiors to the fact that ". . . since the commencement of this rebellion, this woman from her long residence in the capital, her superior education, her uncommon social powers, her very extensive acquaintance among, and her active association with, the leading politicians of this nation has possessed an almost superhuman power, all of which she has most wickedly used to destroy the government."

Officialdom ignored this memorandum. Nevertheless, its writer doggedly persisted in his attempt to prove Mrs. Greenhow a spy. No evidence of importance was gathered for quite a while, although he ordered secret service men to keep a record of all those who entered the Greenhow house and assigned others to shadow them when they left. None of the guests led the operatives to any place that could be considered the headquarters of a spy ring. As a result, Major Allen came to the conclusion that the Greenhow house itself was the headquarters of the Confederate espionage network in Washington and decided to inspect the premises himself.

Consequently, one rainy night in August, Pinkerton, accompanied by three of his assistants, crawled through the dripping shrubbery surrounding the Greenhow mansion and hid beside the front steps. Cold and wet, the trio were about to give up their vigil when a young army officer, a captain in the provost-marshal's office, mounted the stairs and entered the house. Beckoning to his companions, Major Allen quickly scurried to the nearest window, bent down, took off his shoes and, by gestures, showed the trio that he wished to stand upon their shoulders so he could observe what was happening inside the room. His assistants boosted him up, but, unfortunately, the blinds were drawn. However, through a tiny slit, the Major saw the young man hand Mrs. Greenhow a tightly rolled map. After chatting for a few minutes, he gallantly bowed and kissed her hand, then she conducted him to the door and he hurried away.

Leaping to the ground, the detective whispered to his comrades, "Go back to headquarters. I'm going to follow that man."

He did—and for the first time since leaving Dundee, Allan Pinkerton, one-time cooper and now head of the United States Secret Service, walked down a street without shoes!

Confident that he was well hidden by the pelting rain, Major Allen followed his quarry. However, the young officer soon realized that he was being shadowed. Suddenly, he darted into a doorway. Before the detective realized that the captain had vanished, a squad of soldiers with fixed bayonets rushed out of the building and surrounded him. They roughly dragged the sleuth inside, threatening him with their bayonets when he struggled against them, and shoved him into an office. As the secret agent recovered his balance, he saw the man he had been following seated behind a desk, brandishing a revolver.

Leaning forward, the officer demanded in a loud voice, "Who are you? What is your idea in following me? Where are your shoes?"

"My name is E. J. Allen, sir, and I wasn't really following you, sir. You see, I'd lost by way in the rain and was hoping to catch up to you so that I could ask directions. As for my shoes, you—"

"Stop your lies!" thundered the captain. "I've no time to listen to such nonsense. Guard, take this man downstairs and lock him up!"

Thrown into a cell holding several other prisoners, the bedraggled head of the secret service sat shivering in a corner. Finally, he began to warm up and soon noticed that, although most of the soldiers on duty seemed disinclined to have anything to do with the prisoners, one sentry appeared to be a friendly type of man. Cautiously feeling his way, Pinkerton began talking to him and, before long, had succeeded in bribing him to take a message to Scott when he went off duty.

Upon receipt of the note, Scott had Pinkerton brought to his office in the War Department "for questioning" and, as a joke, specified that he be accompanied by an armed guard who had orders to shoot to kill if their prisoner made any attempt to escape. The sergeant in charge told this to Pinkerton, who gravely assured him that he had no intention of trying to get away.

When the detail delivered Pinkerton to Scott, the latter dismissed them and jokingly asked, "Isn't it rather difficult for the head of the secret service to get arrested?"

However, his good humor quickly vanished as Pinkerton related what had happened the previous evening. When the detective had finished his account, Scott called for an aide and commanded him to inform Captain Ellison that he was to report immediately to the office of the assistant secretary of war. Pinkerton and Scott talked about Mrs. Greenhow while they were waiting for the officer to arrive. Upon being told that Ellison was waiting to see him, Scott suggested that Pinkerton step into an adjoining office, but to leave the door slightly ajar so that he could hear all that was said.

Pinkerton had barely slipped out of Scott's office when Ellison entered. The young man drew himself up, stood stiffly at attention, saluted smartly and asked respectfully, "You sent for me, sir?"

"Yes, Ellison, I did. Stand at ease. I think you can help me. I'm very curious about the arrest of that shoeless man last night. If you could give me the details, I would appreciate it."

Ellison was glad to explain everything. He told Scott that he had been visiting friends and while returning home had noticed, despite the driving rain, that he was being followed by a footpad. Therefore, instead of walking directly toward his residence, he had deliberately set a trap by leading the man to the door of one of the barracks maintained by the provost-marshal.

"That's very interesting," commented Scott. "Thank you for telling me all this. Now, I've just one more question. Tell me, did you, or did you not, visit any enemy of the Union last evening?"

"Certainly not, sir," retorted Ellison indignantly.

"Captain, don't you think you've forgotten something?" asked Pinkerton as he entered the room. "We all know you visited a lady who has openly admitted that she favors the South."

As soon as Ellison was hauled off to prison, secret service agents thoroughly searched his quarters. It did not take them very long to discover a mass of evidence that indicated he had been supplying military information to the Confederacy through Mrs. Greenhow for a long time. Upon hearing this, Major Allen was jubilant. He detoured only long enough to recover his shoes, then went up the front stairs of the Greenhow house to see the woman who had mocked him for many months. However, she was not at home.

A servant informed the detective that Mrs. Greenhow was, as usual at that hour, taking a walk. Anyone who watched her as she strolled slowly through the streets of Washington would get the impression that she completely ignored the men and women she passed. In fact, her companion the morning Pinkerton went looking for her, a member of a foreign legation, was positive that Mrs. Greenhow was so completely captivated by his conversation that she had eyes for no one else. Actually, Mrs. Greenhow was looking all about as she chatted gaily with her escort, for, while the angle at which a washerwoman held her basket of freshly laundered clothes or the way a man carried his folded newspaper had no significance to the diplomat, they and other simple signals were code messages that the spy understood.

Just as her friend bowed and politely thanked her for the pleasure of her company and turned to leave, Mrs. Greenhow saw Pinkerton approaching. Quickly, she crumpled a message written in cipher that she was carrying in her pocket and swallowed it, realizing instinctively that she was about to be arrested. Actually, she was not surprised to see the head of the secret service, as she had been expecting arrest for several days—yet she had continued to supply Richmond with information, instead of stopping her activities, in hopes that she might be left alone. She did this in spite of the fact that the warning of her arrest had come from a very reliable source—one of General McClellan's staff had given her the news. The same high-ranking officer had forewarned Mrs. Greenhow that the secret service was also planning the arrest of William Preston, former minister to Spain, for treasonable activities. Characteristically, Mrs. Greenhow had advised Preston to flee to Richmond, but remained in the capital herself.

Just as Pinkerton was about to overtake Mrs. Greenhow, one of the feminine members of her network of spies happened to pass her. Guardedly motioning her colleague not to stop, the head spy managed to whisper, "Watch from the corner. I think they are going to arrest me. If they do, I'll raise my handkerchief."

A few seconds later Pinkerton reached her side. "Good morning, Mrs. Greenhow," he greeted her, gallantly raising his hat. "I arrest you for conspiracy against the United States Government!"

"How dare you say such a thing, Major Allen!" Mrs. Greenhow demanded, drawing herself up proudly. "That's a ridiculous statement and I refuse to take you seriously."

As she spoke, the crafty woman took out her handkerchief
and dabbed her forehead. Then, in unwilling response to
Pinkerton's gentle pressure on her arm, walked slowly
toward her house with head held high.

Still protesting her innocence and flying into a rage
when Major Allen's most capable secret service agents
rushed in and "search was made everywhere," Mrs. Greenhow repeatedly cautioned the head of the secret service
that he was overstepping his authority and warned that
he would suffer for "this outrage." Paying no attention to
any of her threats, Major Allen stationed a guard outside
the house, in hopes of trapping other members of the spy
ring who might come to report to Mrs. Greenhow. The
guard was useless. Little Rose, Mrs. Greenhow's daughter,
who was as loyal to the South as her mother, climbed a
tree near the sidewalk and chanted, over and over, "Mother's been arrested, Mother's been arrested" until she was
pulled down.

Inside the house, Mrs. Greenhow wanted nothing so
such as a few minutes of privacy. Ever since her arrest
she had been desperately trying to find some way to destroy a second message she still had in her pocket because
it was far too bulky to swallow. Finally, Mrs. Greenhow
managed to convince her guards that she had to change
her clothes. They allowed her to go into her bedroom and
she tucked the incriminating note from Richmond into
the top of one of her stockings, feeling that, when she
was searched, no one would ask her to remove it. She was
right. Major Allen's female agent who examined her clothing forgot to look at her stockings!

For over a week secret service agents searched the
Greenhow house under Major Allen's direction. They
found a mass of papers and other documents that proved
without a doubt that Mrs. Greenhow was the head of the

Confederate spy ring in Washington and her house was its headquarters. Still, Major Allen was not satisfied. He insisted that his operatives piece together the half-burned papers in the stove. They were, as he expected, letters from Confederate leaders in Richmond. However, when he showed them to Mrs. Greenhow and asked for an explanation, she insisted that the writing was not a cipher, but merely some of Rose's scribbling.

Because Major Allen had ordered that Mrs. Greenhow's arrest be kept as secret as possible, some of her associates came to Sixteenth Street innocent of the fact they were walking into a trap. Some were released after being questioned and searched by secret service agents. It did not take long for the wily Mrs. Greenhow to observe this and she took advantage of it to send messages to Richmond, despite the fact she was confined to her house. Followed from room to room by a guard, she deftly eluded him one day, slipped into the library and pulled down from a shelf a book stuffed with important papers that had been overlooked by the searchers. She then passed the papers to a woman friend who was being allowed to leave the house. They were carried past the guards concealed in the lady's stockings.

Meanwhile, Major Allen was busy investigating other persons suspected of treason, including William Smithson, a Washington banker, who concealed news of troop movements in business letters; several ladies who wrote to a correspondent in Baltimore "in whose possession interesting correspondence might, no doubt, be found"; also F. M. Ellis, who had built up a profitable business selling bank-note paper to the Confederate Government through an arrangement with the secret service, and then double-crossed Major Allen, who called Ellis "one of the most dangerous men who could be found."

Because he had no operatives in Washington whom he could spare to guard Mrs. Greenhow and he could not call in any of his agents that were working behind enemy lines, Major Allen turned Mrs. Greenhow over to the military authorities, with the understanding that they would see that she was brought to trial. This was not done, however, and she continued to have all the privileges of a person under house arrest. The military used her residence, now known as "Fort Greenhow," to quarter several other women who had been found guilty of spying for the Confederacy. A constant watch was maintained over all the prisoners—particularly Mrs. Greenhow—nevertheless, cipher messages from Sixteenth Street continued to reach Richmond.

In order to find out how military secrets reached "Fort Greenhow" and the means by which they were transported through the Federal lines, several women, loyal to the North, were "planted" in the house, but they learned absolutely nothing of value. In fact, most of the methods used by Mrs. Greenhow to gather information while confined to her home and constantly guarded were never satisfactorily explained. Later, Mrs. Greenhow bragged about her skill in outwitting her jailers in her book, *My Imprisonment, or the First Year of Abolition Rule in Washington,* published in London in 1863. In this fascinating volume she reveals that one of her tricks was to sit in front of a window facing the street and work on a tapestry. "I had," she wrote, "a vocabulary of colors, which though not a very prolific language, served my purpose."

There was no doubt that Mrs. Greenhow seized every opportunity to keep the South informed of Northern plans while in custody. For example, somehow she learned that a group of her friends was being deported to Richmond and decided to use them as messengers. Since she was allowed to take a daily walk accompanied by armed guards in order to get exercise, she purposely strolled by their house, where one of them sat in front of an open window. Reaching into her reticule, Mrs. Greenhow drew out a ball of yarn and tossed it to her friend. "Here's the ball of yarn you left at my house," she called out; "I know you need it."

Four days later, Jefferson Davis unwound the ball and found a cipher message inside.

Little Rose, who was allowed to play on the sidewalk in front of her home by the kindly officer of the detail in charge of "Fort Greenhow," also conveyed messages to couriers for her mother. This went on for several weeks, but, finally, one of the notes the child passed to a Confederate scout was intercepted. As it was written in cipher, the message was turned over to the secret service and, eventually, Major Allen discovered the key. Using the same code, he sent false information by a double agent—a spy who sells information to both sides—to Richmond, but, for some reason, it was never acted upon. However, about the same time, Mrs. Greenhow transmitted material the Southern side did use—a copy of McClellan's personal map and a long list of military maneuvers!

Meanwhile, traitors in high positions and misguided friends of Mrs. Greenhow were agitating to have her released. She added to the confusion by smuggling a letter to Secretary Seward out of "Fort Greenhow"—along with duplicate copies for the newspapers—protesting her "illegal arrest" and the "unwarranted search of my house." Major Allen tried vainly to convince officials that, if Mrs. Greenhow could send a letter to the secretary of state without any of her guards being aware of it, she also could easily pass along Federal military information to the South. Few people bothered to listen to him.

This lack of concern made Allan Pinkerton indignant. He was also openly critical of the manner in which the soldiers assigned to watch Mrs. Greenhow carried out their duties. However, he accomplished nothing beyond learning that, spy or not, Rose Greenhow had influential friends in the city of Washington.

Never in all of his forty-one years had Allan Pinkerton been so angry or as determined to prove he was right. He insisted that the daily walks be stopped and saw to it that little Rose was no longer allowed to play on the sidewalk, but that was all he accomplished. Then, a blockade runner was captured by a Navy patrol boat and, when its cargo was examined, letters addressed to a Colonel Empty were found. To Major Allen, this was obviously a "cover name" and he spent hours rereading the stacks of papers his agents had removed from the Greenhow house. Eventually, he came upon correspondence from a Colonel Michael Thompson. "That's it," he cried. "Empty—from his initials, 'M' and 'T.' "

Feeling that he now had a tight case against Mrs. Greenhow and could convince anyone who came to her defense that she was a spy, Major Allen asked Scott to have the army turn "Fort Greenhow" over to the secret service. As soon as this was done, the major tightened security measures—one agent was severely reprimanded for failing to examine every flower in a bouquet sent to Mrs. Greenhow before allowing her to have it—and gave orders to round up all known Confederate couriers and suspected spies.

Once again, the secret service searched the Greenhow mansion. Although they had previously removed every scrap of paper that might possibly have been used by the wily spy, they found nearly as much incriminating material as they had discovered during their first search. This meant that Mrs. Greenhow had not stopped her activities at all. Major Allen took the copies of what were presumably top-secret documents to the War Department. After a heated discussion, it was finally agreed that, if Mrs. Greenhow could secure such important data and ship it South while under house arrest, the wisest thing to do was to transfer her to prison.

The doors of the Old Capitol Prison clanged behind Mrs. Greenhow on January 18, 1862. Three months later, she was tried for treason before a special commission. Accused of holding "communication with the South," she stoutly maintained that it was only natural that she should do this because she was a Southerner. When asked how she had transmitted messages to Richmond, Mrs. Greenhow curtly replied, "That is my secret."

An extremely hostile witness, she warned her judges repeatedly, "Jefferson Davis will soon hear of this mock trial," and demanded to know, "If Mr. Lincoln's friends give me so much information, am I to be held responsible?" Despite her attitude, the commission promised Mrs. Greenhow her freedom if she would take an oath of allegiance to the United States. This offer was bluntly rejected. The commission then sentenced her to be deported to Richmond. However, McClellan, at Major Allen's request, asked that her exile be postponed. Some of the finest operatives in the secret service had been unmasked in Richmond and their chief feared that Mrs. Greenhow might have testimony that could be used against them during their trial.

Finally, on the last day of May, 1862, Mrs. Greenhow and Rose were taken to Baltimore and, after being passed through the lines under a flag of truce, arrived in Richmond on June the fourth, where they were warmly greeted by Jefferson Davis.

Far from content with what she had already accomplished for the Confederacy, Mrs. Greenhow became a courier and ran the blockade to deliver messages to John Sidell and James Mason, representatives of the Confederate Government in London and Paris, who were to become the central figures in the famous *Trent* affair. In France, Mrs. Greenhow was received at the court of Napoleon III—who afterwards proposed to Seward that the North recognize the South as victorious. She was also presented to Queen Victoria in London.

While advancing the Confederate cause in England, Mrs. Greenhow became as socially prominent as she had been in prewar Washington. Therefore, no one was surprised when she announced her engagement to a peer.

In August, 1863, after promising to return to her fiancé in a few weeks, she left England on the *Condor,* a blockade runner making its maiden voyage to Wilmington, Delaware. Unfamiliar with American coastal waters, her captain ran the vessel aground at the mouth of Cape Fear River. Federal warships and the batteries at Fort Fisher opened fire on the helpless craft and Mrs. Greenhow and two other Confederate agents asked to be set ashore. They went over the side in a small boat, which capsized in the heavy surf. Unable to keep afloat because of the weight of the gold coins she had strapped to her waist, Major E. J. Allen's greatest wartime foe sank beneath the waves.

"The real war will never get into the books."
—Whitman

As INDICATED, during the two years that Major Allen
had matched wits with Mrs. Greenhow he had also
carried out frequent missions for Simon Cameron, Lincoln's first secretary of war, as well as for his immediate
superior, General McClellan. Both men relied upon him
implicitly, as did Stanton when he took over Cameron's
post. Rarely did any of the three give Major Allen specific
instructions, feeling he was capable of handling any assignment. Therefore, in September, 1861, when Cameron
sent the head of the secret service to Baltimore, armed
with authority to arrest those members of the legislature
who were planning to vote in favor of Maryland's secession from the Union, his orders were simple. They read:
". . . use your own judgment as to time and means, but
do the work effectively."

Among the many things Allan Pinkerton had learned
about military men since coming to Washington with Mc-

Clellan was the realization that they resented the intrusion of any civilian—even though he might hold the rank of a major—in matters concerning their command. Therefore, although it was nearly midnight when Major Allen arrived in Baltimore, he went directly to military headquarters and reported. The major then asked to see the commanding general, as he was the bearer of a personal letter to him from the secretary of war. After reading Cameron's message, the general proposed that the provost-marshal send out details and arrest the men named in the major's orders.

Taking great pains to express his appreciation of the officer's willingness to co-operate, Major Allen tactfully suggested that it might be better to conduct simultaneous raids on the houses of the legislators and editors of anti-administration newspapers very early the next morning. "In that way, sir," he pointed out, "we will catch them napping, for they all will be in bed."

Fortunately, the general overlooked the major's bad pun and agreed to his suggestion. Not a man escaped the raids and, heavily guarded, the prisoners were taken in separate carriages to Fort McHenry—whose bombardment in the War of 1812 inspired Francis Scott Key to write "The Star-Spangled Banner." This was Major Allen's scheme to prevent the arrested men from concocting a story in their own defense. Having completed his mission, the head of the secret service, as always, wrote a lengthy report covering every aspect of the assignment. In this one he called Cameron's attention to the fact that "he construed the orders to search for and seize correspondence of a treasonable nature in the possession of the parties arrested, a sufficient warrant for me to enter and search the editorial and press rooms of *The Exchange* and

The South, which I did, seizing the correspondence found there."

Besides learning, during his stay in Washington, how sensitive military men were about their prerogatives, Major Allen had, from bitter experience, discovered that government clerks were extremely careless with documents and correspondence. Therefore, he painstakingly made copies of all the letters he had seized and sent these to the War Department with his report. At the same time, he informed Cameron that he was "retaining the originals in my possession subject to your orders."

Whenever he could get away from personally carrying out assignments from the War Department or engaging in counter-espionage activities in Washington, Major Allen carefully prepared reports based on his own experiences and material sent him by operatives for his good friend, former client and immediate superior, General McClellan. While the major willingly took orders from anyone who had authority to give them, he much preferred to work for McClellan. The general, on the other hand, had, according to Richard Rowan, perhaps the world's greatest authority on spies and the art of espionage, "a voracious appetite for intelligence reports."

Therefore when Major Allen informed McClellan of troop movements and the building of fortifications or passed on the news his operatives had gathered in Confederate encampments, "Little Mac" paid close attention. Never a man of daring action, the General usually heeded such warnings as "the rebels are in possession of accurate drawings of the whole of the defenses at these points, corrected daily when necessary," and postponed any planned change of strategy.

Major Allen personally gathered some of the facts and figures that he passed on to McClellan—while scouting

along Antietam Creek, the scene of one of the bloodiest
battles of the war, his horse was shot from under him—
but the great amount of military intelligence came from
former Agency employees who, like their chief, had
stopped chasing criminals and become spies. Experts in
trailing bank robbers, they were, however, rank amateurs
in espionage.

Looking back, it seems remarkable that Major Allen's
unit accomplished as much as it did. Its members had no
pertinent training and they often took foolhardy risks.
The same operative who questioned a traitor in Washington might very well meet the same individual a few weeks
later when posing as a loyal Southerner in Richmond.
Moreover, military authorities frequently ignored the data
collected by the secret service.

Of all the employees of Pinkerton's National Detective
Agency who joined Allan in government service, none was
more capable as a spy than Timothy Webster. He charmed
Southern belles, impressed both privates and generals and
convinced casual acquaintances and suspicious provost-
marshals that he was a loyal son of the South. He even
won the esteem of Judah P. Benjamin, secretary of war
for the Confederacy.

Yet, Webster had his share of narrow escapes. Once, in
Clarksville, Tennessee, a large body of Confederate soldiers hospitably escorted him to the station to show their
high regard for "the true and loyal son of the South who
had been so kind to them." While this gesture proved to
the secret service agent that his masquerade was succeeding, it also called him to the attention of a doubting member of the local Safety Committee, who wondered why
Webster was so friendly with soldiers and if he had really
come from Baltimore as he claimed.

Webster was on his way to Washington to report to his

chief and the first stage of his journey took him to Memphis. After registering in a hotel, he went upstairs to his room to change his clothes. On returning to the lobby, he found that the vigilante had followed him from Clarksville. A past master at the art of shadowing others, Webster knew all the tricks of losing a "tail." He let it be known that he was on his way to Chattanooga—actually, his destination was Kentucky—to visit a brother whom he had not seen in over twelve years. Major Allens' crack operative loudly demanded a ticket for Chattanooga in the railway station, but showed little interest in getting to his destination quickly. He kept changing from one train to another. However, this ruse failed to confuse the man who was following him. The counter-spy's interest in Webster was so apparent that, strangely enough, the secret service agent was frequently warned by fellow passengers that he was being trailed as a suspected Northern spy.

Eventually, Webster managed to outwit his shadow. At a junction point, he asked the stationmaster for the name of the best hotel in town and pretended he would spend the night there. His shadow, lurking in the background, hearing the conversation, started directly for the hotel. Webster, on the other hand, darted behind a pile of baggage and reboarded the train just as it pulled away. The rest of his trip was without incident and he soon was reporting to Major Allen.

After listening to Webster, the major ordered him to Baltimore, where the operative became well-known to secessionists as a good man to know if you wanted a letter carried to friends in Washington.

Following one such trip, Webster was accosted by William Ziegler, one of the leaders of the mob that had stoned Massachusetts troops as they passed through Baltimore in the early days of the war. Ziegler demanded, "Where were you last night?"

"In Washington, delivering messages, everyone knows that," Webster replied.

"Yes, but they don't know you delivered them to the Yankee secret service headquarters!"

"You're a liar, Ziegler!"

Screaming with rage, Ziegler drew a knife and lunged at Webster. The agent deftly turned aside, drew his gun and snarled, "Get out of here, before I kill you!"

Webster's reactions to Ziegler's charge were so typical of a hotheaded secessionist that all the bystanders who had observed the incident felt that the Northern spy was one of them. This conviction was strengthened in the weeks that followed, as Webster was always willing to slip through the Federal patrols and carry letters to Southern sympathizers in Washington. Before delivering them, however, he gave them to Major Allen to read.

As a trusted messenger of the Confederacy, Webster was soon the bearer of a safe conduct pass issued to him by Judah P. Benjamin, Confederate secretary of war. The pass made it possible for him to move all through the South without fear of being arrested by local Committees of Safety and completely eliminated any suspicion that he was working for the Yankee secret service. It also brought him an invitation to join a secret organization known as the Knights of Liberty.

Webster accepted and a few nights later was led blindfolded to his initiation, where he took a solemn oath to defend the Confederacy and was given the order's password, "Long Life to Jefferson Davis." The Knights, Webster was informed, intended to send 10,000 armed men against Washington from the north, while Confederate troops stormed the Federal capital from the south.

This information, along with his usual package of letters, was delivered to Major Allen by Webster on his next trip to Washington. Both men agreed it was imperative to locate the place where the arms were stored that the invading Knights would carry when they attacked the capital. Webster was sure he would learn the hiding place within a few days and hurried back to Baltimore.

Yet, in spite of the fact that Webster became a very active member of the Knights, the leaders of the organization kept their storehouse a secret. Therefore, the spy held another conference with his superior and they decided to devote their attention to destroying the order. Their scheme consisted of having Webster recommend two men "who could be trusted" for membership in the Knights—they were actually Pinkerton operatives—and have them serve as guards outside the closed doors behind which the plotters held their meetings. After this had been arranged, Major Allen prepared to spring his trap. At the next meeting of the group, Webster made an impassioned speech about the wrongs the South had suffered at the hands of the Yankees and painted a glowing picture of the vengeance that would be wreaked on the North. Just as he referred to "the smoking ruins of Washington," the room was filled with Federal soldiers whose officers had, by Major Allen's orders, waited to hear these words sounding through the doors kept slightly ajar by their guardians before entering. Most of the Knights were hauled off to prison, but a few escaped. Among them was Webster. To his Southern acquaintances, who did not know that his escape had been arranged, Major Allen's favorite spy was more of a hero than ever.

Nevertheless, Webster was arrested in Baltimore and by Union authorities! His association with known seces-

sionists had attracted the attention of a Federal agent and
he was taken into custody as a suspected Confederate spy.
Unknown to the arresting officer—Major Allen preferred
that the true identities of members of his staff be concealed from even their associates in the secret service—
and fearing that, if he told Agent McQuayle who he was,
his usefulness as a spy would cease, Webster said nothing.
However, while imprisoned, he managed to send Major
Allen a simply worded telegram that meant nothing to his
captors, "Is Tim all right?"

In Washington, the chief of the secret service did not
have to reach for the code book to decode Webster's telegram. It was obvious that his top agent was under Federal
arrest in Baltimore. The canny detective realized that he
had been presented with a wonderful opportunity to en-
hance his operative's reputation, so he spent several hours
carefully composing a reply to Webster's message which
he dispatched to the provost-marshal. It ordered that
Webster be transferred to Fort McHenry. Major Allen
stressed that as many people as possible should learn this,
but warned that his guards should be the only ones that
knew the agent was to be allowed to "escape." The major's telegram outlined what he wanted done down to the
smallest detail and, among other things, made it absolutely
clear that the guards were to shoot in the air as their
prisoner ran away and not *at* him.

Everything went according to plan. Webster "escaped"
amid a salvo of shots and made his way back to Baltimore,
where he was hidden by Southern sympathizers. The next
day, the city buzzed with Webster's latest exploit, just as
Major Allen knew it would. Newspapers featured his escape on their front pages. The pro-Union *American* had
this to say about "the unfortunate incident."

ESCAPE OF A STATE PRISONER

It was rumored yesterday that the man Webster, who was arrested, stopping at the hotel of Messrs. McGee, upon the charge of being concerned in the regular transportation of letters between Baltimore and the seceded States, had succeeded in making his escape. It is learned upon the best authority that during a late hour of the night he was removed from the western police station and placed in a carriage under the charge of a special detective officer. The wagon was driven toward Fort McHenry, he having been previously ordered to that post, but while the vehicle was in motion, he gave a sudden bound from his seat, and before the officer could seize him he was beyond his grasp. It is not known which direction he took, but he will scarcely be able to escape from the city.

Unlike its rival, the *Gazette,* which openly supported the South, was positive that no agent of the Federal Government could hold Webster captive. It ended its account by boasting, "We have reason to believe that Webster is beyond the reach of the Yankees."

As a matter of fact, Timothy Webster, outstanding detective and master spy, was by now safe in Washington, reporting to Major E. J. Allen.

Upon his return to the Confederacy, Webster was more popular than ever. He now began the most dangerous months of his career as a spy, serving as a double agent under Major Allen's direction. In so doing, Webster risked his life constantly to provide his superior with information that would bring the war to an end. Eventually, bedridden in Richmond—he had been ill for some time, but stubbornly refused to rest—he was unmasked. After a trial held in his sickroom, he was sentenced to be hanged.

When Major Allen heard of the fate of "the bravest man

I ever knew," he hurried to the White House. President
Lincoln, who knew and admired Webster, immediately
called a special meeting of his Cabinet to discuss how the
Federal Government could save the spy's life. After hours
of discussion it was finally decided that Secretary Stanton
should write a personal letter to Jefferson Davis, calling
attention to the fact that no Confederate spies had ever
been hanged by the North. Stanton wrote the letter and
closed it by hinting that, if Webster were executed, this
policy would be changed. As soon as the secretary signed
his name, the letter was handed to a courier who boarded
a flag-of-truce boat and sailed for Richmond. At the
same time, a copy of the letter was telegraphed to Jefferson Davis. Both letter and telegram were ignored. Early
in the morning of April 29, 1862, Timothy Webster, "Spy
of the Rebellion," died on the gallows.

*   *   *

Although extremely popular with the rank and file under his command and liked by many newspapermen, General McClellan was a disappointment to those who had
hoped for an early end to the war. Actually, "Little Mac"
spent more time drilling his troops than leading them in
battle. Moreover, he always insisted upon having vastly
superior forces before engaging in even a simple skirmish.
McClellan's constant requests for more troops prompted
Lincoln to comment, "Sending that man reinforcements
is like shoveling flies across the room."

Cautious by nature, the Union commander was also
restrained from launching offensives by Major Allen's
estimates of enemy strength. One typical report reads:

I have the honor to report the following information . . .
which has been extracted from current statements made

here by spies, contrabands, deserters, refugees and rebel
prisoners of war . . . it is unnecessary for me to say in the
very nature of the case, guarded as the rebels have been
against the encroachment of spies . . . it is impossible
to ascertain the specific number and character of their
forces. . . .

In conclusion, Major Allen submitted his estimate of the
strength of the Confederate forces facing McClellan, and,
as he frequently did in his reports, added a warning that,
in all probability, his figures were low.

Despite his feeling that he did not have enough men
for the operation, the widespread cry of "On to Richmond!" rang so loudly in McClellan's ears that he was
forced to undertake the Peninsular Campaign. His plan
was to transport the Army of the Potomac, consisting of
the men he had drilled so well, to the eastern end of the
Yorktown Peninsula, and make his thrust at Richmond
with the York and James Rivers on his flanks. This meant
marching through a rough and, in many cases, unmapped
territory.

Although McClellan commanded the largest army that
had been assembled in the United States up to that time,
his strategy was to advance slowly and use artillery and
siege guns to blast a path to the Confederate city. Unfortunately, the Southern generals refused to fight defen-
sively. Under "Stonewall" Jackson, Confederate troops
hit the Army of the Potomac repeatedly, ruining McClellan's "perfect paper plan." Moreover, spring rains had
brought brooks and rivers to flood level, adding to the
difficulty of marching across the Peninsula. The flood waters of the Chickahominy separated two of McClellan's
corps from his main forces and the Confederates, led by
General Johnson, attacked them and won the battle of
Seven Pines.

Although the Union should have suffered far greater losses than it did at Seven Pines, two major developments resulted from the clash of the Blue and the Gray on that day. General Lee replaced Johnson, who had been seriously wounded, as commander-in-chief of the Confederacy and General George McClellan demanded more troops.

Meanwhile, "Little Mac" failed to take advantage of several opportunities to inflict serious damage on the enemy. Finally, disgusted at his military leader's vacillation and knowing that the general public was alarmed at the administration's failure to bring the war to a successful conclusion, Abraham Lincoln decided to remove McClellan from his post of commander-in-chief. The president soon discovered that reaching this decision was far easier than finding a replacement for "Little Mac." When Senator Benjamin Wade of Ohio, who had long pressured Lincoln to get rid of McClellan, angrily demanded his ouster during the Peninsular Campaign, the president asked, "Whom would you put in his place?"

"Anybody!" snorted Wade.

Calmly Lincoln replied, "Wade, *anybody* will do for you, but I must have *somebody*."

Ambrose E. Burnside was Lincoln's eventual choice, but he in turn was replaced, as were several other generals, until the president found his "somebody" in Ulysses S. Grant. The news that McClellan had been relieved of his command created mixed reactions. Even today, military historians are divided on the question of "Little Mac's" military ability. To one man, however, there never was any question. Major E. J. Allen stoutly defended McClellan as an individual, general and presidential candidate. In 1882, long after the guns were stilled, Pinkerton wrote in *The Spy of the Rebellion*—his memoirs of the secret service—that McClellan had acted wisely in the Peninsular Campaign and insisted that accurate figures of enemy strength had been gathered by both himself and members of his staff. There could not have been any possible errors, the detective-turned-author explained, as ". . . from every available field the facts were gleaned. From prisoners of war, contrabands, loyal Southerners, deserters, blockaderunners and from actual observations of trustworthy scouts."

Although Major Allen was well acquainted with General Burnside, having met him through a mutual friend —Allan Pinkerton of Chicago—who did criminal investigation for the Illinois Central Railroad, which employed the general in private life, he had no desire to serve under him. He was both disgusted and distressed at what he sincerely believed to be the injustice done to McClellan. Therefore, he tendered his resignation as head of the secret service to the War Department.

However, Allan Pinkerton, no matter how indignant he might be over Lincoln's treatment of McClellan, was not the type of man to sulk in Chicago when his particular abilities could be used to serve his country. Therefore, a few days after the War Department accepted the resignation of Major Allen, one E. J. Allen became a civilian employee of the government. Allen's assignment was to investigate suspected cases of fraud against the United States and to check on damage claims made against the army. Meanwhile, Allan Pinkerton's younger son, Robert, joined William as a secret service agent. Now all the male Pinkertons were acting as detectives for the government.

Assigned to the Department of the Mississippi in the spring of 1864, to adjust claims for cotton damage, Mr. Allen operated out of New Orleans. Despite the fact that there were active members of the secret service in that city, Secretary Stanton ignored them when President Lincoln disapproved of General Sherman's armistice with General Jackson and ordered that hostilities continue. Stanton asked Allen to undertake a special assignment. In his letter, the secretary explained, "Jefferson Davis and his companions will, no doubt, take advantage of the armistice to escape with his plunder, said to be a large amount of specie." He then requested Mr. Allen to "look out for them and arrest them if possible."

Actually, Davis made no attempt to escape until after the fall of Richmond in 1865. He was captured near the Georgia-Florida boundary line and imprisoned. Although Mr. Allen had nothing to do with his arrest and was no longer connected with the secret service of the United States, he did manage to uncover a plot to free eight thousand Confederate prisoners interned at Camp Douglas, in Chicago. A group of Southern military officers slipped into the city and arranged with local Copperheads—members of a group disloyal to the government and named after one of the most dangerous of American snakes—to supply the prisoners with arms. After releasing themselves, the Confederates planned to seize the undefended city. However, the scheme collapsed and its leaders were arrested because the "loyal Southerner" assigned to distribute the rifles was a Pinkerton agent!

One morning in 1865, Mr. Allen, as usual, rose early and left his New Orleans hotel for his morning walk. As he reached the street, he heard the shouts of newsboys. Although he thought it strange that they should be peddling papers at such an early hour, he paid no attention to their cries. Then, he suddenly realized that they were shouting that President Lincoln had been shot. Frantically waving to the nearest boy, Allen rushed toward him, grabbed a paper and threw him a coin.

Leaning against a lamppost, Allan Pinkerton read with horror how John Wilkes Booth, a member of one of the most famous acting families in the world, had assassinated the president while he was sitting in a box at Ford's Theater. Erroneously, the paper also reported the death of Secretary Seward.

Stunned, all claims for damaged cotton and swindler's frauds forgotten, the loyal detective walked slowly up the stairs to his room. At last he gained control of himself, reached for a pen and paper and wrote the following letter:

> New Orleans, La., April 19, 1865
> Hon. Edwin M. Stanton, Secretary of War:
> This morning's papers contain the deplorable intelligence of the assassination of President Lincoln and Secretary Seward. Under the providence of God, in February, 1861, I was enabled to save him from the fate he has now met. How I regret that I had not been near him previous to this fatal act. I might have had the means to arrest it. If I can be of any service, please let me know. The service of my whole force, or life itself, is at your disposal and I trust you will excuse me for impressing upon you the necessity of great personal caution on your part. At this time the nation cannot spare you.
>
> E. J. Allen

It is most interesting to note that, even though he was under terrific mental strain when he wrote this letter, the sender did not sign it with his real name. Such attention to little details was one of the secrets of Allan Pinkerton's success.

＊   ＊   ＊

Not long after Secretary Stanton received the above letter, Mr. E. J. Allen, like Major Allen, severed his connection with the government. Both had served their country with courage and imagination and, although many of their accomplishments would never be known to anyone save those responsible for recording all aspects of the War Between the States in the national archives, neither wanted credit for what he had done.

In Chicago, Allan Pinkerton resumed active supervision of his detective agency and soon was engaged on some of the most complicated cases of his colorful career that brought him international fame.

12

*"Nothing is so difficult but that it may
be found out by seeking."*
—Terence

ALTHOUGH THEY HAD MISSED their chief's first-hand advice and personal direction, Superintendents Bangs and Warner of the New York and Chicago branches of Pinkerton's National Detective Agency had greatly expanded the firm's operations while Allan was in government service. Their task had not been easy. Most of the Agency's most capable operatives, like their employer, were in the secret service during the war, which meant satisfying old clients and pleasing new customers with only a skeleton force. Pinkerton himself had not worked on a private case in nearly four years—with one exception.

Everything about this case fascinated Allan and it presented a challenge he could not resist. Moreover, it was a very attractive young lady who asked Pinkerton to help her and he found it difficult to refuse. Therefore, Major Allen took a brief furlough from his military duties and enjoyed a vacation, during which he trapped a clever band of swindlers.

While in Clarksville, Tennessee, on a secret service mission, Pinkerton was timidly approached by Elizabeth Redford. Her fiancé, an officer in the Federal Army, had revealed Major Allen's true identity to her. Between sobs, the pretty young lady told Pinkerton of a band of gypsies who had visited the neighborhood. She explained how their queen, a Mrs. Hooker, "who told the most wonderful fortunes," had convinced her father that she was the only gypsy in the entire world who knew the ancient Egyptian secret of causing gold to double itself. The gullible man believed her and, according to his daughter, took his life savings—$15,000—which he had kept hidden in an old clock in the attic, to Mrs. Hooker and begged her to cast her magic spell.

"Mrs. Hooker agreed," continued Elizabeth, "and said that the only reason she would do it was that she had a thousand dollars in gold that she was planning to double and would only have to bother the spirits once. She put her bag of gold coins on the table beside the two leather ones Father's money was in and asked him to move the table close to the window. Then Mrs. Hooker said that they would have to wait until the sun went down as the spirits never appeared in daylight. When it became dark, she began to chant in a low voice and tied the necks of the sacks with a cord to which amulets hung by gold thread. Then she covered them with a brightly colored paper, lit a candle and began chanting very loud. As the candle flickered, she made weird motions with her hands and kept swaying her body back and forth.

"Finally, shuddering as if awaking from a trance, Mrs. Hooker told my father to take all three bags home and hide them in a safe place. She warned him not to look at the bags for sixteen days—one day for each thousand dollars they were to gain, thanks to the aid of the spirits. Father wanted her to take the sack containing her coins, but she insisted that he take care of it for her.

"He did everything she told him to do, hiding the sacks in the old clock under the eaves in the attic. Father waited patiently for the sixteen days to pass, sure that Mrs. Hooker had doubled his fortune—you see, he trusted her because she had given him her gold to take care of during the time it took for the charm to work. Then we found out that the gypsies had left Clarksville and although only fourteen days had passed, Father opened the bags. Mr. Pinkerton, there was nothing inside them but washers, nuts, bits of metal and some rivets! The shock nearly killed poor Father; he's been under the doctor's care ever since."

"I'm very sorry to hear that, Miss Redford," Allan said soothingly. "Now I've one or two questions. Was your father sitting at the table when this so-called spell was being cast?"

"Yes, sir, he was."

"Was the window open?"

"As wide as possible. Mrs. Hooker said something about the spirits being helped by currents of air passing over the sacks."

"That explains everything. Your father was so distracted by the waving of Mrs. Hooker's arms that he didn't see her accomplice reach in the window and exchange the money sacks for duplicates containing worthless metal. Then too, he probably was half asleep, thanks to her chanting, and wouldn't be able to see a great deal by the light of a candle. Well, we know how it was done. Now let's see if we can get the money back and send Mrs. Hooker to prison. The only trouble is, I've been away so long—I don't know if Warner has an operative that can handle this affair."

What Pinkerton really meant was that he did not know whether the short-handed Warner could spare an agent. The Agency always seemed to have someone on the payroll with the special qualifications that were needed during any investigation. This time it was Operative Blake, who had lived with gypsies, knew their ways and had friends in their encampments all through the Middle West —and he could be spared.

Fortunately, Elizabeth Redford had saved the odds and ends of metal substituted for her father's gold and, when Blake arrived in Clarksville, he found a promising clue among them. It was a rivet with a star-shaped design on its head. Steeped in gypsy lore and customs, Blake knew tha every gypsy tinker mended pots and pans with rivets bearing his own personal design. With the rivet in his pocket, Blake set out to find its maker. He was extremely lucky. The man he was looking for was in an encampment not too far from Clarksville and turned out to be an old friend. Brewer readily recognized his trademark—the star-shaped design—and told Blake that he had made several such rivets for Mrs. Louise White, who was, in the tinker's words, "a bad gypsy who gives all of us the reputation of being thieves."

When Blake reported all this to Pinkerton, the chief detective quickly decided that Mrs. White and Mrs. Hooker were one and the same. Tracking her down in wartime with only one or two operatives would have been considered impossible by anybody else. Here, however, a bit of the famous Pinkerton skill paved the way for apprehending the suspect. Rummaging through the ashes and debris of the deserted encampment at Clarksville, Blake found part of a letter and an envelope addressed to Mrs.

Mary Hooker. It was signed "Your cousin, John Stanley" and had been mailed from Bloomington, Indiana.

Drawing on Warner's depleted staff, Pinkerton ordered Operative Edwards to go to Bloomington to find out all he could concerning John Stanley. Edwards learned very little. Stanley no longer lived there. However, the postmaster told Edwards that he was forwarding Stanley's mail to Mitchell, Indiana. Meanwhile, Blake, who had been visiting one gypsy camp after another in hopes of overtaking the woman who called herself Hooker or White, depending upon circumstances, learned from a doctor in Bowling Green, Kentucky, that he had treated the sick child of a gypsy woman named Mrs. King. The name meant nothing to Blake, but he asked a routine question, "What did she look like?"

Before the doctor was halfway through his description, the operative, having asked Elizabeth Redford the same question, knew that the gypsy with the gold ring dangling from her left ear was not only Mrs. King, but also Mrs. White and, sometimes, Mrs. Hooker!

Superintendent Warner, who had been summoned by Pinkerton to help track down the swindling gypsy queen —Allan's theory being the more men worked on the case, the sooner he could resume his military rank—had not been idle all this time. He, too, had gone from one gypsy camp to another, gathering information about the Stanley tribe. Among other things, he learned that their leader had died and the three branches of the family would soon meet to elect a new chief. He had also discovered that one of the candidates for the post was Joshua White, the husband of Mrs. Hooker-King-White.

When Warner told Pinkerton what he had learned, the detective ordered his assistant to assign an operative to watch each group. Blake was greeted as an old friend by the band to which he was assigned, but Operative Edwards, who pretended to be an author looking for background material for his next book, was, at first, curtly refused permission to join John Stanley's camp. However, when Edwards "accidentally" jingled some gold coins in his pocket, he was made welcome. In fact, Stanley barely gave him time to unpack before asking if he would like to play poker. Edwards, an excellent player—despite Pinkerton's rules for operatives—agreed, but insisted that the stakes be gold. Stanley agreed, went to a nearby caravan which was guarded by a husky gypsy, returned with a handful of gold coins and the game began.

Edwards' luck was phenomenal and he won hand after hand. Several times after losing a pot, Stanley would ask Edwards to wait a few minutes while he "went to see Zed." Then he would go to the caravan, argue heatedly with its guard, force his way through the canvas flaps and return with another handful of gold coins. Finally, Zed brought the game to a close by blocking Stanley's attempts to enter the caravan. Edwards didn't care. He was a two-way winner. He had won a considerable amount of money and had also discovered where Redford's gold was being hid and who was responsible for guarding it.

With so many demands upon the Agency, Pinkerton did not have another operative to watch the third branch of the Stanley tribe. He could, of course, have telegraphed Washington and asked that one of his men drop whatever he was doing for the secret service and become a private detective for a few days. But Allan Pinkerton was much too honest a man to use any of his staff on a private case while they were working for the government. Just when it seemed that there was no one available, however, he found the ideal man.

This was a Professor Potts. His title had not been

granted by any college or university, but by custom—all music teachers were called "professor" in those days. A one-time theatrical star, Potts was now a broken-down actor who had been out of work so long that he didn't have the price of a decent meal in his pocket. However, years of wandering up and down the country had given Potts a special faculty for making friends with total strangers. He was delighted that Pinkerton wanted to cast him in the role of a vagabond. It meant money in his pockets and food in his stomach, and his part was not difficult for him to portray. All he had to do, Allan told him, was to join a gypsy band, watch for a kettle mended with star-shaped rivets and try to learn the whereabouts of a woman known variously as Hooker, White and King.

Within a week, Potts was welcome in every caravan in the encampment. Even the often critical Allan Pinkerton could not find fault with the way the one-time actor performed. Not only did Potts find the kettle, but he so charmed Mizella, a beautiful gypsy maid, that she told him all about herself and her family, including her aunt, Mrs. Joshua White, who was in a camp near Calhoun, Kentucky.

When Pinkerton received this information, he ordered Blake to Calhoun. Potts was to continue playing his romantic role with the impressionable Mizella and try to figure out some way to get the gold away from Zed—for Edwards had reported all the details of the poker game. The latter turned out to be quite an easy assignment. Potts sent word to his chief that all the Stanleys were soon to gather at New Harmony, Indiana—where Robert Owen conducted his famous unsuccessful experiment in communal living—and Pinkerton had an operative waiting there when Zed arrived.

The gypsy hired a room in a boarding house and so did

the Pinkerton agent. Waiting until Zed went out, the operative searched his room and found two bags of gold concealed between the mattress and spring of the bed. Upon his return, Zed, despite the fact that he drew a knife and battled fiercely, was handcuffed and jailed.

Zed was not the only one who did not attend the meeting of the Stanley tribe and vote for a new leader. Mrs. Hooker was not even in New Harmony, although her husband was a candidate. She was much too busy in Calhoun, Kentucky, where Ezra Allen, a wealthy old man who acted like a dottering fool, had been begging her for days to cast the ancient spell she had told him about and double his fortune. At last she consented.

It was late in the afternoon when Mrs. Hooker asked Ezra to sit at a table beside an open window. After her victim placed his bag of gold in the middle of the table, the gypsy threw a cloth covered with magical symbols over the bag and then tied a gold cloth around it. For three hours she called up the spirits by muttering Romany phrases. As it became dark, the old man, evidently hypnotized by her voice, fell asleep. When Mrs. Hooker felt sure he was sleeping soundly, she chanted a little louder and a hand reached through the window, removed the cloth-covered bag. A second later, another cloth-covered bag replaced the original one on the table. Then, suddenly, sounds of a scuffle were heard and, without raising his head, the old man called, "Warner?"

"Yes, Major. Everything is under control."

On the way to the nearest jail, Pinkerton delightedly told the gypsy that the gold he had used to trick her was that which she had stolen from Mr. Redford. However, the detective did not bother to mention—probably because he did not approve of card playing—that three hundred

dollars of the original fifteen thousand was missing, while
Edwards' poker winnings almost equaled that amount!

*   *   *

Using Redford's gold to trap Mrs. Hooker appealed
greatly to Pinkerton, for he loved practical jokes. In New
York, during the War Between the States, he was once
approached by "steerers" for a gambling house. "Steerers"
were extremely respectable-looking men who were employed by gambling houses. They would spot an apparently prosperous individual, engage him in conversation
by pretending to mistake him for someone else, and when
told they had made a mistake, act embarrassed. Then, as
any gentleman would do, they would humbly apologize
and offer to make amends by inviting the stranger to their
club—where he soon lost all the money he had in his pockets!

Pinkerton immediately recognized the pair for what
they were and decided to have some fun. "I'm extremely
sorry, gentlemen," he said sorrowfully, "but I can't go
anywhere. You see, I'm in the Quartermaster Corps and
I'm carrying a very large sum of money with which I in-
tend to purchase horses for the cavalry. So you must excuse me. I'd best get back to my hotel."

This made the men more insistent than ever—just as
Pinkerton knew it would—and finally he pretended to be
persuaded to join them. In the gambling house he wandered from one end of the establishment to the other, ignoring the pointed hints of his hosts that he might "like
to have a little fun at the tables." At last, the owner himself, fearing that Major Smith—as Pinkerton called himself—was going to buy horses instead of losing at the faro
table the government funds with which he had been en-
trusted, bluntly suggested that he play.

"Major Smith" evaded the invitation by replying, "This, sir, is one of the finest clubs I have ever seen. My compliments to you. Moreover, I'm impressed by the type of man that belongs to it. I'm sure all in this room are very successful in their chosen profession."

Then, to the gambler's utter astonishment, Pinkerton added, "In fact, I recognized some of them from their pictures. There are two or three well-known forgers here, a couple of lads who have considerable talent opening locked vaults and several—"

"Say, just who are you, anyway?" demanded the proprietor, whom Allan had recognized as Dan Noble, listed in the Agency's files as a professional gambler, expert bond forger and daring bank robber.

"I'm Allan Pinkerton of Chicago, but I doubt if my name means anything to you or your friends."

How wrong he was! The detective had hardly finished speaking before most of the men in the room rushed toward the door. Raising his voice, Pinkerton shouted, "Stop! There is no need for you to break up your games. This was purely a social visit. And now, gentlemen, if you will excuse me, I must leave."

Once they had recovered from the shock of being identified by Pinkerton, the gamblers roared with laughter. They appreciated Allan's joke and poked fun at the "steerers" who had mistaken the famous sleuth for an easy mark.

Pinkerton's love of practical jokes played an important part in the only case the Agency ever handled for a couple who were considering a divorce. Although Francis Warner had patiently explained that Pinkerton's National Detective Agency did not accept divorce work to a would-be client who wanted her husband shadowed so that she could learn the name of the woman with whom he had fallen in love, she insisted upon telling him all the circumstances. Warner, impressed by her story and her obvious love for her husband, became convinced that she was worrying unnecessarily. Therefore, he promised to consult his chief, to see if the long-standing Agency rule against engaging in divorce work could be waived in this case.

Meanwhile, Allan, who relaxed by taking a long carriage ride every afternoon, irrespective of the weather, met the husband, whom he already knew, while driving through the countryside. Pinkerton, always a shrewd judge of character and mood, realized that something was bothering the man and wondered why he was walking along a dusty road miles from Chicago. Allan reined in his horses and invited his friend to join him. A series of discreet questions told the detective what was troubling his passenger. He and his wife had foolishly quarreled over a minor matter and now the distraught man was positive that his wife had fallen in love with someone else and wanted a divorce.

As he talked, Pinkerton became convinced that the only thing that prevented a reconciliation was pride. However, all he said was, "Don't worry. I'll turn around and go back to town and I'll find out just what your wife is planning."

When he reached the Agency office, Pinkerton told Warner that, although he was going to assign an operative to shadow a married woman at the request of her husband, he was sure that the results of the investigation would not lead to a divorce. "You know I wouldn't take the case if I thought my client really wanted a divorce," Allan reminded Warner. Then he told what had happened while he was out driving. When he finished, his assistant burst out laughing and gleefully confessed that he was going to ask permission to have a man shadowed under the same circumstances. He then reported the conversation he had had with the wife.

Instead of calling the couple together and acting as peacemaker, Pinkerton could not resist the opportunity to play a practical joke. "This is what we will do," he advised Warner with a grin. "You send a messenger to the lady, stating that I agreed to have her husband shadowed and, as a result, you have identified the woman he loves and will have her in the office tomorrow afternoon at three o'clock. Tell her that you think she should be here at the same time. Meanwhile, I'll notify my friend that the man his wife loves is coming here at three, and I think it advisable that he come and see him. They'll both be here, never fear."

The next day, the husband and wife entered a private room in the Pinkerton offices by separate doors, but a few minutes later, the couple congenially walked out together and Pinkerton's National Detective Agency maintained its reputation for never engaging in investigations for those seeking evidence to secure a divorce.

* * *

Pinkerton had little time for practical joking in the postwar years, however. He was far too busy directing the operations of the Agency in tracking down swindlers and confidence men, investigating insurance frauds, chasing embezzlers and leading lawmen after train robbers and other outlaws. In fact, he had barely settled down in Chicago after his military service, when, in response to the urgent demands of an old and valued client, the Adams Express Company, he was back in Maryland, reviewing the details of a train robbery that had taken place there on March 18, 1863. Although the Agency had been investi-

Allan Pinkerton keeps in contact with his operatives by a private telegraph line.

gating the robbery for some time, the seven men who had committed it were still at large.

It had been a well-planned crime. Four of the robbers, posing as ordinary passengers on a Northern Central train, had entered the baggage car and beaten the Adams Express messenger into unconsciousness. When the train reached the place where their confederates were waiting, the four threw the safe—which contained nearly $100,000 —out the car door and returned to their seats. Meanwhile, the other three criminals loaded the safe into a wagon and hauled it to the gang's hiding place. Here, they were joined by their four companions in crime, who had left the train at the next stop.

Under the direction of Bangs and Warner, operatives had been seeking the seven men for some time. Pinkerton approved of their actions and ordered that the search be intensified, suggesting that the gang had probably hidden most of the money and then scattered. He was right. Before long, all seven thieves were in jail. Hoping to receive light sentences in return for their co-operation, the robbers disclosed where the loot was hidden.

Pinkerton, who never made compromises with criminals, promised them nothing, but in April, 1865, he handed Sanford bills and bank drafts totaling $84,594.50. In return, the assistant general superintendent of the Adams Express Company gave Allan a receipt. The detective took it back to Chicago and hung it beside the one Sanford had signed when acknowledging receiving the money recovered from Maroney. Curiously, the date on the second receipt was April 10th. The day before, Lee had surrendered to Grant at Appomattox and the War Between the States had ended. But Allan Pinkerton's fight against crime was just beginning.

*   *   *

Because so much publicity was given to cases solved by Allan and the men he directed, the general public sincerely believed that "The Pinks"—a nickname given to the Agency by criminals—never failed to carry out an assignment successfully.

This was not true. Maximilan Shinburn, master safecracker and escape artist extraordinary, outwitted the Pinkertons completely. Allan ruefully admitted he was the only criminal that ever escaped from his operatives. A brilliant student in college, fluent in five languages, Shinburn had decided as a young man that he could get rich much faster by robbing banks than by working in them. Therefore, he began to study locks and safe combinations with far greater interest than he had shown for any of his courses in college.

Before long, Shinburn was an expert locksmith and knew more about bank vaults than most financiers. However, once in a while as he went about visiting banks under the cover of darkness, entering them with false keys, Shinburn would encounter a safe he found impossible to open. When this happened, he would, if possible, buy a similar model and practice until he could swing its doors open as easily as if he were using a key. Combinations were usually no trouble to Shinburn. A mechanical genius, he had invented a rachet-like tool that enabled him to discover the proper sequence of numbers to which the dial on the lock should be spun.

He was just as clever in escaping from jail. Sentenced to serve ten years for robbing a bank in Concord, New Hampshire, Shinburn made an impression of the lock on his cell with mashed potatoes, then fashioned a key from a spoon stolen from the prison dining room that fitted it perfectly. Therefore, when false keys were used to enter the vault of the Lehigh Coal and Navigation Company, at

White Haven, Pennsylvania, on the night of July 9, 1868, Pinkerton, who had been given the case, informed his client that Shinburn had been responsible for the theft of the missing $56,000.

Allan was correct in his assumption and, eventually, "The Pinks" took Shinburn into custody. The next step, according to accepted Pinkerton policy, was to turn the criminal over to the prosecuting authorities for trial. However, in this particular case, the Lehigh Company did not want Shinburn jailed until he had returned the money in exchange for a promise of a light sentence. Although Allan made no secret of his dislike for such an arrangement—it was against his sense of justice—he finally consented to hold Shinburn on suspicion of bank robbery, rather than bring him to trial while the details of the compromise were worked out by representatives of his client and the prisoner.

Although Pinkerton refused even to consider bargaining with Shinburn, he did make one promise. When the time came for the master criminal to be tried, Pinkerton operatives would bring him into court. The detective took a suite in a Wilkes-Barre hotel in which the constantly handcuffed Shinburn and a detail of Pinkerton men lived as a not-too-happy family. For five days and nights, one operative or another remained shackled to Shinburn and he was never left unguarded.

Even Allan Pinkerton was positive that Shinburn could not escape. But he did! At night, as he lay on the bed, fully dressed, beside his sleeping guard, the thief, using his left hand, picked the lock of the handcuffs with his tiepin and walked quietly out the door of the suite to freedom!

Realizing that the Pinkertons would waste no time tracking him down, Shinburn, under an assumed name, shipped as a seaman aboard a tramp steamer bound for Belgium. Once in that country, he was safe even from Allan Pinkerton, as Belgium had no extradition treaty with the United States at that time. Yet, Shinburn soon gave up freedom from arrest to return to the United States in order to rob a few carefully selected banks. It was not that he needed money in order to live—he had netted $200,000 in one Connecticut robbery alone—but in Belgium he had met a penniless baron who wanted to sell his title. The price was high, but Shinburn was confident he could pay it, thanks to his skill with locks.

Actually, Shinburn robbed but one bank in order to become a baron, but it was a criminal masterpiece. Under his direction, a band of clever crooks stole $786,879 from the Ocean National Bank, in New York City. They first rented part of the bank's basement where, as they smoothly informed the curious, they planned to establish the local branch office of the Chicago Life Insurance Company. However, they went on to explain, it would be several weeks before the branch would be open for business, due to the fact that, under the laws of New York State, insurance companies chartered elsewhere had to meet certain legal requirements. While there was no doubt that their firm would get a license, it would take time.

Shinburn and his accomplices were evidently outstanding confidence men as well as experts in the art of bank robbery to satisfy the bank officials with this explanation, for the bank asked for no references nor did they make any inquiries about the Chicago Life Insurance Company. If they had, they would have found that the only place it existed was in Shinburn's fertile imagination. Moreover, it seems strange at this date that the bank would be willing to lease its cellar to anyone. One thing is sure, nobody connected with the Ocean National—from office boy to president—had any of Allan Pinkerton's innate curiosity. Otherwise he might have wondered why the tenants spent most of their time inside the bank, instead of getting their office ready.

Actually, the "office" was ready and it opened for business late one Saturday afternoon, long after the last employee of the bank had gone home. It was a most unusual opening—a large hole in the basement ceiling and in the floor above! Thanks to their hours of observation inside the bank, when Shinburn and his associates in crime wiggled through the hole, they were directly in front of the vault.

The whole operation had been so carefully planned that it was dark by the time the robbers were inside the bank. Quickly, they hung black oiled silk sheeting over the doors and windows, to prevent any passer-by from seeing them in the light of the lanterns that they had kept hidden in their "office." Shinburn opened the massive steel doors of the vault without any difficulty, because, by some unexplained means, he already knew the combination!

The inner locks presented no problem to the skilled safe-cracker either. With the aid of a huge jack, hoisted from the room below, and a kit of several hundred burglar tools, Shinburn crushed, pried or opened every device that was supposed to protect the funds of the Ocean National Bank. Although they had an entire weekend in which to work, the robbers made their haul in less than a day and escaped. Because of their weight, they left behind the jack and some thirty thousand dollars in gold coins. Why they also abandoned "one of the most complete and costly collections of burglar tools ever assembled" is still a mystery.

With his share of the loot—probably the largest, since he had planned and directed the robbery—Shinburn was on his way to Belgium before the robbery was discovered. The money he brought with him was given to the bankrupt nobleman and Shinburn, the bank robber, lived royally and "honestly" for the rest of his life as Baron Shinburn.

Baron or not, Pinkerton would have brought him back to the United States for trial, if possible. However, there was no legal way in which this could be done because of the lack of extradition treaties between this country and Belgium. Incidentally, despite the existence of such agreements between the United States and other nations, Pinkerton operatives had, by one means or another, brought wanted men back to America from Asia, Africa, Europe and the South Seas.

For years, Pinkerton, who had been instrumental in bringing about collaboration between several states so that they turned wanted criminals over to one another for prosecution, had urged that the Federal Government sign such agreements with foreign countries. The Shinburn case, among others, finally made his voice heard in Washington, and the United States signed extradition treaties with several other nations. In them, the various governments promised to refuse to grant asylum to criminals who had fled to another country in order to avoid arrest.

Shinburn's escape was most unusual. Pinkerton was always willing to spend huge sums of money and employ dozens of operatives in order to maintain the Agency's reputation because he was justly proud of its excellent solved-case record. Nevertheless, there were times, as in the Ocean National Bank case, when he had to admit that his firm had failed to satisfy a client. Practically every operative on the payroll of the Agency's Chicago office was assigned to find William Pinkerton's terrier which had dis-

appeared, yet the pup was never found. The memory of
their unsuccessful search for the missing pet was the
greatest source of embarrassment to "The Pinks" until just
a few years ago, when the New York branch applied for
permit renewals for four hundred pistols.

In checking their arsenal to make sure the correct serial
numbers were listed on the application, Agency officials
discovered that nine of their guns were missing! As Pinkerton's National Detective Agency had closely co-operated with civil law enforcement agencies ever since its
founding, the disappearance was immediately reported to
the New York City Police Department. Despite the seriousness of this loss, it did have a comical aspect. Detectives were assigned to investigate a robbery in the world's
best-known detective agency, and a thirteen-state alarm
was issued for the guns! However, as a reporter for the
New York *Times* wrote: "The Pinkertons were able to
save face, though, because the public eyes had no more
success tracking down the pistols than the private eyes."

13

"I do not understand: I pause: I examine."
—Montaigne

A LOST DOG, an escaped criminal and some missing guns stand out in the history of Pinkerton's National Detective Agency for just one reason: they are among the very few cases the firm did not bring to a successful conclusion. Perhaps the main reason why his organization rarely failed a client was Allan's insistence that a criminal be trailed until he was captured, tried and convicted. While "The Pinks" frequently solved cases quickly, thanks to the vivid imagination of their chief, many an assignment was brought to an end only by months of persevering, watching and waiting.

Another reason why the Agency was particularly successful in solving bank robberies and train holdups and in apprehending forgers, was the completeness of its files. Started by Allan before the War Between the States, these records—forerunner of the modern police department's rogues' gallery—were crammed with material to identify criminals long before Alphonse Bertillon introduced his methods. This famous French anthropologist—a specialist in the study of mankind—later suggested a system of identifying people through measurements, coloring and fingerprints. Pinkerton's files not only recorded the physical characteristics of thousands of known criminals, they also noted each subject's methods of operation on a card that contained his biography and a photograph. For years, until the establishment of the Bureau of Criminal Investigation by the F.B.I., Pinkerton's files were the only source of such information. Even today, when tracking down criminals is no longer the Agency's most important activity, there are 1,500,000 identification cards in the files.

Pinkerton was one of the first law-enforcement officers to recognize that each criminal has his own technique, whether he robs a bank or forges a will. He explained how he used this knowledge to solve cases to a Chicago bank president in 1880: "In my thirty years of detective work these things have become so marked and fixed that, on reading a telegraphic newspaper report of a large or small robbery, with the aid of my vast records and great personal experience and familiarity with these matters, I can at once tell the character of the work, and then, knowing the names, history, habits, and quite frequently the rendezvous of the men doing that class of work, am able to determine, with almost unerring certainty, not only the very parties who committed the robberies, but also what disposition they are likely to make of their plunder, and at what points they may be hiding."

The Pinkerton files were constantly consulted by law-enforcement officials until the Bertillon system came into general use after being introduced in the United States by the city of Chicago—and the Pinkertons—in 1886. In fact, even after they established their own criminal iden-

Detective Mendelsohn and Superintendent Bangs arrest an escaping criminal.

tification bureaus, many police departments still called
upon the Agency for help because its files not only gave
the usual information about a criminal, but also described
his background, companions and possible hide-outs. Moreover, "The Pinks" never removed a card from their files
because the person it described had not committed a recent crime—Pinkerton's National Detective Agency never
considered a case closed until the criminal was declared
dead officially.

Besides allowing various police departments to use the
Agency's files, Pinkerton also co-operated with banks all
over the country by sending them information gleaned
from his cards. These frequent bulletins described robbers or explained various new techniques used by yet
unidentified criminals so that bankers could take precau-
tionary measures. He also advised the manufacturers of
safes that his files revealed that certain of their models
were easy to open with burglar tools. Sometimes he even
offered suggestions as to how the safes should be rede-
signed.

No authority ever questioned the accuracy of the data
in the Agency's files. When Harvey Logan, one of the leaders of The Wild Bunch—"the largest, toughest, and most
colorful of all western gangs" and the last criminal in this
country to escape from prison on horseback—was shot by
a posse, the sheriff did not recognize him. The bulletin he
sent out merely reported that an unknown outlaw had
been killed after holding up a Denver and Rio Grande
train and described the dead man. James McParland, who
was in charge of Pinkerton's branch office in Denver, compared the information in this bulletin with material in
the Agency files and then flatly stated that the dead man
was Logan.

Although McParland was recognized as the man who

knew more about western outlaws than anyone else in the country, his identification of Logan was disregarded. Moreover, when a bank in Cody, Wyoming, was robbed some weeks later and the leader of the gang was said to be Logan by the bank employees, McParland was openly ridiculed.

William Pinkerton, as proud of the Agency's files as his father, decided to send Lowell Spence, assistant superintendent of the Chicago office, who had trailed Logan with such persistence that the outlaw had sworn to kill him, to look at the body of the train robber. Spence had the dead outlaw exhumed and after one glance said, "That's Logan." However, local authorities still refused to believe that they had shot the notorious desperado. Spence changed their minds by handing them the file card on Logan. They found that the description written on it tallied in every respect with the appearance of their "unknown train robber."

Despite his files and ability to turn clues into convictions, Pinkerton often found it extremely difficult to get criminals sentenced after they had been apprehended. This was particularly true in the West, where juries hesitated to return a vote of guilty in cases involving well-known outlaws, because they were afraid they might be shot by friends of the prisoner or members of his gang. Moreover, in many communities, the police were corrupt and refused to honor the evidence that Pinkerton operatives presented when requesting the arrest of a suspect. In some cases, "The Pinks," knowing that local authorities would not co-operate with them, forced their captives to accompany them to another city where the police were known to be honest.

Typical of the alliance between crooks and lawmen was the businesslike arrangement between Piper, perhaps the greatest forger who ever lived, and certain police chiefs all over the United States. If Piper "pulled a job" in the area under their jurisdiction, they received a percentage of the profits. Moreover, it was understood that, if "The Pinks" came to a town where this mutual agreement had been set up, Piper had the unique privilege of being arrested under a false name on a bogus charge and kept in jail until they left.

Although Piper began his criminal career in the United States, he soon operated on an international scale. By raising the value of bills of exchange in Paris and Cuba, he amassed a large fortune. Upon his return to this country, he greatly increased this by daring speculations in cotton, operating a hotel in St. Louis and a host of other enterprises. However, he lost everything in the Panic of 1857. Piper more than recouped his losses in the next ten years. According to Pinkerton's calculations, this skillful penman defrauded business establishments out of more than a million dollars during that period.

This would have satisfied most forgers, but not Piper. He devised one of the most daring schemes in the history of crime—the stealing of the 400,000 pounds of gold stored in the closely guarded vaults of the Mexican Government.

Technically, the gold belonged to France. In 1864, Louis Napoleon, then emperor of France, anxious to rebuild the empire won and lost by his uncle, Napoleon Bonaparte, landed troops in Mexico. Had it not been for the War Between the States, the Federal Government would have prevented this under the Monroe Doctrine, which affirms that the United States will regard as an unfriendly act any move by a European nation to interfere in the affairs of, or increase its possessions in, the Americas. However, the nation had no military forces to spare as General Grant began the final phase of the conflict between the North and the South.

Just as his uncle had set up puppet kings and emperors in the lands he conquered, Louis Napoleon offered the throne of Mexico to Ferdinand Maximilian Joseph, archduke of Austria, who assumed the title Emperor Maximilian I. Racked by internal strife, Mexico was in a turmoil and the people gladly accepted the ruler from overseas, hoping that his reign would bring peace. However, neither Maximilian nor his wife Carlota pleased anyone and, under the leadership of two Mexican patriots, Juárez and Diaz, rebellion broke out in 1866.

Piper knew that Maximilian realized his life was in danger and felt that he had been deserted because France had withdrawn its protective troops. Therefore, the forger reasoned, the abandoned ruler would welcome anyone from Paris who might advise him. After counterfeiting documents that described him as a secret agent of the French Government, Piper, bearing forged letters presumably written by officials in the Paris treasury to Maximilian, went to Mexico with three confederates who were to help him transport the gold.

When they arrived in Brownsville, Texas, the men heard that Juárez and Diaz were meeting practically no opposition and that it was only a matter of time before Napoleon's protégé would be dethroned. Because they were afraid that they might be killed if they continued on to Mexico City, Piper's companions deserted him, but he went on alone.

After presenting his forged credentials to Maximilian, he imperiously demanded that the French gold be turned over to him at once. The emperor, awed by his air of authority and the documents he carried, ordered a count of the stored gold to be made, but did not set a definite date for it to be handed over to Piper. Meanwhile, the revolutionary army was drawing nearer and nearer to Mexico City and Piper realized that it would be physically impossible for one man to transport the gold out of the country. Regretfully, he abandoned his plot and fled. Three days later, Benito Pablo Juárez, the rightful president of Mexico, resumed his office and Maximilian was captured, tried and shot.

Back in the United States, Piper resumed his forging of checks, deeds, wills and bills of exchange. He also did a thriving business in changing the numbers on bonds stolen by other criminals so that they could sell their loot. In 1869, "The Pinks" trapped Piper in Vermont and he was sentenced to serve ten years in prison. Granted time off for good behavior, he was released, seemingly reformed.

Shortly after leaving prison, Piper had a long talk with Pinkerton. During their conversation, the master forger told Allan the full story of his career and assured the detective that he was "going straight." Pinkerton gave Piper some money and wished him luck—as he so often did to those he had placed behind bars upon their release from prison. Yet despite his good intentions, Piper found it impossible to lead an honest life and resumed his criminal activities, but he died penniless.

Helping reformed criminals was a Pinkerton family trait. William Pinkerton not only aided many men he had sent to prison upon their release, in addition, he frequently supported their families while they were in jail. Allan's older son was also among the first advocates of the parole system in the United States. Called Big Bill by criminals and Billy by his friends, the son was, in some respects, a far better detective than his father. His brother Robert, the more popular of the two because he was not as reserved as William in dealing with employees, was also an outstanding sleuth, having, like William, served his apprenticeship in the secret service.

William and Robert had to work longer and harder than any other employees on the Agency staff, for the senior Mr. Pinkerton wanted no charge of favoritism leveled against him. Therefore, his sons, like any operatives, took and obeyed the orders of Bangs and Warner. Nevertheless, Allan was proud of his sons' ability. Writing of the capture of those responsible for robbing an express car on the Mobile and Ohio Railroad, he said, "William A. Pinkerton was the person having immediate charge of the matter, and to his energy, perseverance, and sagacity is mainly attributable our success."

The Pinkerton brothers often investigated crimes as a team. Assigned to a case involving a train holdup, they found that the express messenger, Morrell, had been so severely wounded by the robbers that he was unable to speak. After some discussion, the doctor agreed to let them see Morrell, but warned them that he was in very poor condition, due to the fact that he had been shot twice with a thirty-two caliber revolver. Both Pinkertons immediately knew what that meant—the holdup had been an amateur job, professionals used a thirty-eight. While they were pondering this fact, the doctor reminded them not to let Morrell say a single word. "Remember," he urged, "he still has a bullet in his lung."

True sons of their father, the Pinkerton brothers devised a scheme by which the injured messenger could describe the men who had shot him. "Don't try to talk," William warned, "but listen carefully. We're going to ask you some questions. If the answer is 'yes,' press my hand, if it is 'no,' squeeze my brother's."

By this unique system of communication, William and Robert not only worked out the way the robbery had been committed, but also learned that it was the work of four masked men. Moreover, Morrell conveyed the information that two of the men, despite the fact that their faces were covered, gave him the impression that they were twins. Most remarkable of all, the messenger, by pressing and squeezing the detectives' hands, told them that one of the twins lisped!

*   *   *

Even though Allan Pinkerton was fortunate in having such competent sons, resourceful assistants in supervisory positions and a staff composed of men and women of great ability, he probably never would have taken a voluntary vacation. However, he was forced to rest when he suffered a slight stroke in 1869. Advised by his doctor to go to a health resort at Springville, Indiana, he soon became bored and restless. As soon as he could, he returned to Chicago and the beloved routine of the Agency office.

Although his physical condition was much improved, Pinkerton no longer personally rushed from one section of the country to another in response to telegraphic appeals for assistance from the firm's clients. Gradually, he began to rely more and more on William and Robert, but he still supervised all Agency activities, although he did forget business long enough to take two trips to Glasgow. Nevertheless, whenever the firm was retained to investigate a particularly complicated case, Allan insisted upon taking an active part in the operation. Therefore, despite doctor's orders to remain in Chicago, he hastened to New York City after reading a telegraphic report of George Bangs' investigation of an express car robbery. Within hours after his arrival, Allan Pinkerton was involved in one of the most curious cases of his career.

14

*"Curiosity is one of the permanent and certain
characteristics of a vigorous mind."*
—Johnson

W E'RE HERE! So open up! Come on, in there, open
up!" shouted the foreman of the gang assigned by
the Merchants' Union Express Company to unload the
baggage car attached to a limited train that had just pulled
into New York City's Grand Central Station from Chicago.

When the sliding side door of the car did not open in
response to his command, the foreman pounded on it and
yelled at the top of his voice. Still there was no response.
Knowing that he could not open the door from the outside, the foreman asked the train crew to see what was
the matter. They forced their way into the car through
another locked door opening off a vestibule between the
baggage car and a day coach.

When they broke in, they saw that the car's two large
safes that had contained nearly $200,000 in cash and ne-
gotiable securities were open and as empty as a schoolyard

149

on a Saturday afternoon. Moreover, there was no sign of John Putnam, the baggagemaster. Then a brakeman noticed a slight movement under a buffalo robe in a corner of the car. He lifted the robe and found Putnam, tied tightly with heavy cord. His face was streaked with blood and a froth-covered gag covered his mouth. An ambulance was hastily summoned and the barely conscious baggagemaster was rushed to the hospital.

George H. Bangs, who had risen from his post as head of the New York City branch of Pinkerton's National Detective Agency to become the firm's general superintendent, and Francis Warner, in charge of the Chicago office, went to see Putnam in the hospital. Although suffering a great deal of pain, he was not seriously injured and was able to tell the two detectives what had happened.

"After we left Albany—the last stop before New York— I had nothing to do," he told Bangs and Warner, "so I decided to take a nap. I often take one, that's why the robe is in the car. Anyway, I curled up in the robe on top of some crates and soon fell asleep. Some time later, when we were outside Poughkeepsie, I awoke with a start."

"What caused that?" demanded Bangs.

"Two masked men, dressed in black—like undertakers —were bending over me," Putnam continued. "They stuck a gag in my mouth and then began to tie me up. I struggled, but one of them picked up an iron bar and hit me on the head, knocking me out. I didn't begin to come to until after we had reached New York."

While his chief assistants were interviewing Putnam, Allan Pinkerton was inspecting the baggage car. His keen eyes soon discovered that the edge of the sliding door had been whittled away near the hook on the inside, which, when dropped into a staple, made opening the door from the outside impossible. Closer examination revealed that the whittling had been done with a knife which had two nicks in the blade.

Turning to an official of the Merchants' Union Express who had accompanied him to the freight yard, Pinkerton requested, "Have somebody remove this door and then store it in a safe place. I'll want it for evidence when I find the person who did the whittling."

"How will you know he is the one you want?" queried the official. "Won't it be difficult to prove?"

"Not if he owns a knife that has two knicks in the blade," was the confident reply.

Poking about in one of the corners of the baggage car, Pinkerton found a small bit of brass shaped roughly like a hook. At first, the detective thought that the thieves had used it to enter the car. His theory was that they had inserted it in the whittled space and used it as a lever to open the inside lock of the sliding door. However, when Pinkerton tried to open the door with the piece of brass, he was amazed to find that nothing could slide by the whittled section. "That's strange," Allan muttered to himself and examined the door again. He finally decided that the carving had been done from the inside of the car and not from the outside. "What I can't understand," he ruefully admitted to the representative of his client, "is why anyone on the inside would bother to whittle the side of the door."

Neither could Pinkerton explain why a sliver of white soap was caught in the tight curls of the buffalo robe, although he had a hunch that it was an important clue. However, neither the knife marks nor the soap impressed the directors of the Merchants' Union Express Company, for, even though Putnam's doctor reported that he had just missed suffering a fractured skull, they were convinced that the messenger was lying. He had, they told

Pinkerton, admitted the robbers to the car, helped them open the safes and then allowed himself to be gagged and tied in order to make his account of the robbery seem plausible. Nor did the directors change their minds about Putnam when Bangs, after questioning the train crew, learned that two men had left the train when it slowed down for a signal in the Bronx. No particular attention was paid to them because it was a common practice for passengers who lived in upper New York City to risk their lives and jump off at this point, rather than ride all the way downtown. However, as one of the passengers stopped under a street lamp, a member of the train crew had idly noted that he wore dark clothes and carried a suitcase.

"That may be so, Pinkerton," commented Putnam's employers when the detective reported what the members of the train crew had told Bangs, "but how do you account for the fact that the robbers entered the baggage car without forcing the door to the vestibule?"

"They could have done it by either of two ways," Allan replied. "They might have secured an impression of the lock on the vestibule door months ago and made a key to fit it, then waited until they learned, by one means or another, that a valuable shipment was to be carried in the car. The other way, which I think is much more likely, Putnam may have closed the door, but neglected to make sure that the lock snapped. Putnam, himself, admits that this is possible."

"If he admitted everything, it would save a great deal of trouble," snapped one of the express company men. "You'll have Putnam followed everywhere he goes, won't you?"

"I will if you insist, but I wasn't planning to, because I am sure that having Putnam shadowed isn't going to lead us to the stolen money. If anything unlocks that mystery, it will be this little bit of brass on my desk."

The piece of brass was a mystery in itself. No member of the Pinkerton staff had any idea what it was, nor did it even resemble anything any of the operatives had ever seen. In order to identify it, Allan had his men call on every manufacturer of, and dealer in, brass in both Chicago and New York. Not one of them had any idea as to what the fragment was or who had made it.

Meanwhile, other Pinkerton detectives went from one end of the Bronx to the other, in hopes of finding someone who had seen the two men who had jumped off the Chicago Limited. Their search was also unsuccessful. Then, as Superintendent Bangs walked by a music store one afternoon, his eye was caught by an attractive display of accordions in the window. He stopped, peered through the glass and saw that, on the more expensive models, the keyboard was fastened to the rest of the instrument with a small, hook-shaped piece of brass. Hurrying back to the Agency office, he told his chief what he had seen.

Pinkerton was elated. "I think you have solved our puzzle. Now here's what I want done. Have operatives check every firm that repairs musical instruments in both Chicago and New York. We know it's extremely likely that our piece of brass came from an accordion and anyone that planted it in the baggage car to confuse us will want to replace it as soon as possible. Therefore, I want the names and addresses of everybody who has had an accordion repaired recently in either New York or Chicago."

Bangs knew just the operative to assign to the job, for, as usual, Pinkerton's National Detective Agency had an employee with the special qualifications needed to gather even this particular kind of information. This time it was a member of the New York staff who was musically inclined. Any other detective would probably have confined himself to checking the repair orders handled by well-known shops on busy streets, but Bangs' choice for the task knew dozens of out-of-the-way places where professional musicians went to have their instruments repaired. After "checking out" the well-known shops, the operative began calling on the little-known ones.

After trudging up and down long, steep stairways in dozens of tenement houses in the slums, the detective finally located an elderly repairman in the teeming East Side who remembered repairing an accordion whose brass fastening piece was missing. Because he did not have another of brass, he had replaced it with a copper hook.

Unfortunately, the old man had absolutely no idea as to who his customer was, or his address. "I do a cash business," he explained, "so I don't keep any records. Someone brings me an instrument to fix and I do it. When they come for it, they pay me. All I can tell you is that a lady came here with an accordion one day and called for it the following day. I never saw her before or since."

The detective asked a routine question, "What kind of a lady was she?"

"She was, well, what you'd call elegant," the repairman responded, his wrinkled face breaking into a beaming smile. He then went on to describe the fine silver fox furs which his customer had been wearing and said he had noticed them particularly because the day was so warm. Gentle but skilled prodding by the operative stimulated the old man's memory. A great deal of what he said was of no value, but several important facts came out of his ramblings. The woman was a very pretty brunette, about thirty-five years of age, who obviously had been quite upset that the accordion was not ready when she called for it. "I remember that she begged me to hurry and finish the job," the repairman told the detective, "as it was getting near suppertime and she said she had twenty people to feed. Then, while I was working on her accordion, she walked up and down the room, looking at the various instruments that I had to fix. She took a violin off the wall and played a short piece. She played very well, mister."

Everything the old repairman had said was written down and turned in to Pinkerton by the operative. After reading his agent's report, Pinkerton laid it aside, puffed vigorously on his cigar for a while, then spoke to Bangs. "Well, we know more than we did. First, somewhere there is an accordion with a copper fastening instead of the original brass one. Second, this accordion was taken to be repaired by a woman who is, providing the old man's opinion can be trusted, beautiful, brunette and a musician. Those are all the facts we know, but let's make some guesses—of course, they will be all wrong if our lady had a legitimate excuse for having the accordion repaired. Now let's see . . . evidently our suspect runs a boarding house—not an inexpensive one because her furs show that she must have money. Probably it's one of those brownstone institutions that take in paying guests, one of those places where people who dislike hotels and want to feel they are living in a private home, board. I'm still guessing, but I'd say she must operate a rather large establishment because she told the repairman that she had 'twenty people to feed.' "

"Just a minute, Major!" Bangs injected. "Have you any idea how many people in the city of New York take in paying guests? How are we going to know where to look for this mysterious woman?"

"I really don't think it's going to be too difficult to find her because I figure that she couldn't carry a heavy accordion very far from where she lives. Let me have a map of the city and I'll see if I can locate her house."

While Bangs had tremendous respect for Pinkerton, he just could not believe that his employer could look at a map of New York City and then say, "The woman we're looking for lives at such and such a place." However, he took the requested map from a filing cabinet and handed it to Allan.

Pinkerton studied the map for hours. Finally, he decided that the nearest section to the East Side that had exclusive accommodations for paying guests was Waverly Place. Operatives sent to that pretentious neighborhood soon discovered that one of the most fashionable residences for paying guests in the area was operated by a woman named Mrs. C. E. Barret, who was beautiful, brunette and an accomplished violinist. Moreover, her silver fox furs were the envy of nearly every other woman in the district.

Allan ordered Mrs. Barret shadowed, but she did nothing to excite suspicion. Operatives reported that she seemed a woman of charm and culture and that she had recently given a violin concert for a group of musically inclined residents of Waverly Place. Pinkerton's agents also learned that, while none of the residents of Waverly Place had ever seen Mr. Barret, they all knew that he was a traveling salesman.

On the surface, there was absolutely nothing to indicate that Mrs. Barret was anything else than what she appeared to be—a cultured woman whose boarders were respectable citizens. Nevertheless, Pinkerton was not satisfied. Always a curious man, he wanted to know why Mrs. Barret had taken her accordion to the slums to be repaired. Was it only because it was the nearest place, or was it because the old instrument maker kept no records?

Until these questions were answered, the great sleuth reserved his opinion of Waverly Place's most attractive landlady.

One of Pinkerton's favorite means of securing information was to direct an operative to become friendly with a suspect and gain his confidence. In his memoirs, he repeatedly points out that such a technique was distasteful to him but "the course pursued was the only one which afforded the slightest promise of success; hence its adoption. Severe moralists may question whether this course is a legitimate or defensible one . . . but the office of the detective is to serve the ends of justice; to purge society of the degrading influences of crime; and to protect the lives, property and the honor of the community at large; and in this righteous work the end will unquestionably justify the means adopted to secure the desired result."

Pinkerton chose one of his most attractive and talented female operatives, Mrs. Katherine Brelsford, for the assignment of finding out the truth about Mrs. Barret. He had, at first, considered "planting" a man in the Waverly Place boarding house, but changed his mind when it occurred to him that Mrs. Barret might have arranged for the accordion to be repaired for a man who, she knew, had taken part in the robbery. If this were the case, Mrs. Barret would be far more likely to confide in a woman.

Pretending to be Mrs. Catherine Smithers, a widow from Los Angeles who supported herself by giving French lessons, Mrs. Brelsford applied for a room at the boarding house. Pinkerton had known that she would have to give Mrs. Barret references, therefore, the operative was prepared when asked for them. They spoke of Mrs. Smithers in the highest possible terms. They should have, as Allan had forged them himself!

After reading the references, Mrs. Barret said that she

would be delighted to have Mrs. Smithers for a paying guest and was happy that she happened to have a room that was vacant. She was, however, not half as happy as Pinkerton's agent was when she found the room was next to that of Mrs. Barret, on the second floor. This made it comparatively simple for the operative to make an impression on Mrs. Barret and, in less than two weeks, they were intimate friends.

For about a month Mrs. Brelsford kept a careful watch on her landlady, but learned nothing that was of any value to Pinkerton, to whom she reported daily while pretending to be looking for a position teaching French. Fearing that Mrs. Barret might become suspicious of her failure to get a job, the "French teacher"—as she was known to the other boarders—complained of the lack of interest in foreign languages in New York City and expressed her disappointment in not finding work.

"Don't worry, my dear," Mrs. Barret consoled her, "you'll find a position shortly, I'm sure. Right now, all you need is cheering up. Come on, let's have some music."

Going to the piano, Mrs. Barret played for several minutes. When the detective complimented her, she brushed the praise aside by saying, "You should hear my husband —he's a traveling salesman and isn't home much. He plays the piano and the accordion beautifully."

"The accordion! I've always wanted to play one," exclaimed Mrs. Brelsford. "I can play the piano, although not half as well as you do, but I have never tried the accordion."

"You can try it right now," said her hostess and left the room. In a few moments she returned with an accordion. The Pinkerton operative did not have to pretend delight when she saw the instrument, for a quick glance told her that it was the one that had been repaired by the old

man on the East Side, as all its fittings were shiny brass
except for a copper hook that held the keyboard in position.

When Mrs. Brelsford told Pinkerton about the accordion, the master detective was positive that Mrs. Barret's
husband was involved in the robbery of the Merchants'
Union Express Company car. "What I'd like to know is
his whereabouts," he told his charming assistant. "I have a
feeling that Barret has no intention of coming back to
New York, although he may be staying out of town only
until he thinks investigation of the robbery has been
dropped. At any rate, try and get his address."

Mrs. Brelsford explained that, ever since renting the
room in Waverly Place, she had sought to check the post-
marks on her landlady's mail. "I haven't had a chance,"
she admitted. "You see, sir, all letters are delivered to each
roomer's door by one of the maids."

"Keep trying," Allan urged. "Our whole case depends
upon finding Barret."

Several days later, just before the maid was due to distribute the mail, Mrs. Brelsford knocked on Mrs. Barret's
door and complained of a headache. Mrs. Barret was very
sympathetic and graciously offered to give her some pills
that might dull the pain. While she was getting them, the
maid arrived. Acting as if she wanted to save Mrs. Barret
the trouble of opening the door, the operative quickly
opened it, took the single letter brought by the maid and
promptly handed it to her landlady. As she did so, however, her trained eyes read the postmark. The letter was
from Toronto, Canada.

When Mrs. Brelsford called at the Agency office to
make her daily report and told Pinkerton about the postmark, his comment was cautious. "The chances are that
the letter was from Barret—although we can't be sure—

because Canada is a logical place for him to hide. He probably knows that he is more or less safe there under our present extradition treaty. Unfortunately, it doesn't cover all crimes."

Upon her return to Waverly Place, Mrs. Brelsford was greeted by a maid who said, "I've got a note for you from the missus. She got a letter from her husband and has gone away."

Hoping that it contained valuable information, the lady detective tore open the envelope. She was disappointed. All the note said was that Mrs. Barret had been called away suddenly and that she had no idea when she would return to New York City. Meanwhile, management of the boarding house would be under the direction of the housekeeper, a most capable person.

* * *

While Mrs. Brelsford was living at Waverly Place, other Pinkertons were questioning hundreds of people in the Bronx, in the hope of finding someone who had seen the two men who had reportedly hopped off the train on the day of the robbery. Pinkerton had carefully instructed his operatives merely to ask the person to whom they were talking if he had seen any suspicious characters in the Bronx about the time the Chicago Limited arrived. Nothing, Allan stressed, was to be said about two men leaving the train.

Day after day, the operatives reported that they had found no one who had seen anything that might help solve the case. Yet the interviews went on, and Pinkerton's men were getting weary of their assignment, when John Burns, a laborer, told his questioner, "Yes, I saw two men the morning that express car was robbed. In fact, I saw them jump off the train."

Because nothing had been said to Burns about the men leaving the train, Pinkerton knew that Burns was telling the truth. Therefore, he listened intently as the laborer said that, after leaving the Limited, the two men walked toward him and passed under a street light. This gave him a chance to see that they were dressed in black, "like undertakers"—the same phrase that Putnam had used to describe the robbers' clothing. One of the men, according to Burns, was middle-aged and very distinguished-looking because of his neatly trimmed Vandyke beard. His companion was a much younger man and he was dark, handsome and mustached.

Pinkerton had a meeting with the directors of the Merchants' Union Express Company following his interview with Burns. When all the officials were comfortably seated, Allan startled them by saying, "Gentlemen, we have a description of Baggagemaster Putnam's confederates in the robbery and have reason to believe that they are in Canada."

"Putnam? Why, you led us to believe that he was innocent," exclaimed one man in astonishment.

"Pardon me, sir, but I didn't. I merely pointed out how the baggage car could be entered without any collusion on his part and—"

"Why, then, did you tell us that, although you would have detectives shadow Putnam, you were positive that they would report that he had done nothing to indicate he knew anything about the stolen money?" interrupted another member of the group.

"For a very simple reason—I knew that Putnam was smart enough to know that he would be watched and therefore would do nothing suspicious. Frankly, gentlemen, I've been convinced almost from the day I accepted this case that Putnam was involved."

"We all felt that way too, but had no proof. How did you decide he was one of the robbers?"

"It was the fantastic story he told Superintendents Bangs and Warner that convinced me. You will recall that he said he went to sleep right after the train left Albany and slept soundly until awakened suddenly by two masked men."

"That sounds as though it could have happened. I don't see why you call Putnam's story fantastic," complained another official of the express company.

"You're absolutely correct—but Putnam claimed he was awakened when the train was just outside Poughkeepsie. Now, gentlemen, let me point out that, if he had been fast asleep before being awakened and slugged unconscious almost immediately thereafter, he couldn't have any idea where the train was. No lights were on in the car, nor does it have any windows. Moreover, the train hadn't made a recent stop so that he might figure out where the attack took place."

"Don't forget, Pinkerton, Putnam's been on the Chicago-New York run for years. He must know every curve, hill and bump in the roadbed."

"That makes no difference. No one who has been in a deep sleep and is suddenly awakened knows how long he has been sleeping. Add to this the fact that, in the few minutes between his waking up and being knocked out, Putnam had two masked men bending over him. No man in such circumstances would have the slightest idea where he was."

"How about the lump on his head and the fact that he was frothing at the mouth?"

"They are easily explained. That froth was nothing but lather made from the sliver of soap I found in the car. As for the bump on Putnam's head—well, that had me fooled for a while. It was an expert touch and certainly made Putnam's story seem truthful. Actually, I don't think his partners meant to hit him so hard, but that lump on Putnam's head made me believe him until I stopped to think that he never could have known where the attack took place."

* * *

Although Pinkerton had sent warning bulletins to every bank in Canada, alerting them to watch for anyone attempting to sell the securities stolen from the express car as soon as he learned from Mrs. Brelsford about the letter postmarked Toronto, no immediate attempt was made to dispose of them. Evidently the robbers were content to wait until they had spent the large amount of cash they had taken before trying to market the bonds.

All Pinkerton could do was wait. Then, three months after the robbery, a young man giving his name as John Martin offered to sell a bank in Hamilton, Ontario, $4,000 worth of bonds. Martin seemed a respectable citizen and the bank agreed to buy the securities. However, because the Agency had sent out a stream of bulletins to remind banks and stockbrokers to watch for the stolen bonds, an official of the bank engaged Martin in conversation while clerks compared the numbers of his bonds with those listed on the Pinkerton circular. Their check revealed that Martin's bonds were among those that had been stolen from the baggage car. The police were called and the young American was arrested.

As soon as Pinkerton heard what had happened, he sent Bangs to Hamilton. Bangs talked to Martin in his cell and heard what seemed to be a legitimate reason why he had had the bonds in his possession. Martin explained that he had met two men in Toronto—his descriptions of them were identical with those Burns had given Pinkerton of the pair who had jumped off the train—who sold him the securities at an excellent discount because they had to leave for New York City early the following morning, before the banks opened.

Despite his native caution and Pinkerton training, Bangs was inclined to believe Martin, but decided to check his background. A famous American surgeon, when asked if he knew the young man, replied, "I certainly do and I don't know a finer person."

Pinkerton's chief assistant was now convinced of Martin's innocence. He went to the jail to tell him so, but just as he was about to ask permission to see the suspect, a lawyer entered claiming he represented Martin. Bangs immediately changed his mind. Definitely something was wrong. He knew that Martin had not asked for a lawyer. Then why had one come to the jail? Probably more important was to know who had sent him? Bangs had no answers to these questions, but he soon learned that the attorney was a most capable individual. Shortly after his visit, Martin was released on the grounds that it was impossible to prove that he knew the bonds were stolen.

Bangs had Martin's lawyer shadowed day and night. In Toronto, he led his "tail" to a building that housed a famous restaurant on the first floor and an elaborate gambling establishment on the second. The operative could not follow the attorney to the gambling rooms because he did not have one of the cards that would serve as a ticket of admission. These were issued by the owner to a limited number of patrons only. Curious as to the reason why the lawyer visited the gambling den, Pinkerton decided to send an operative to Toronto with orders to secure one of the hard-to-get cards.

As usual, there was an operative on the staff with the necessary special talents to mingle with Toronto's sporting set. Like Allan, Operative Adams knew all about race horses. Therefore, he let it be known that he was a gambler from Massachusetts and soon he was well-known to frequenters of the casino.

One night, as the detective was seated at the faro table, he spotted a man with a Vandyke beard who answered the description Burns had given of one of the pair he had seen in the Bronx. Casually, Adams asked a fellow-player the name of "that distinguished-looking gentleman" and learned it was Edward Stewart. Covertly watching the suspect, the detective saw him beckon to the lawyer who had effected Martin's release from jail, and the two retired to a corner, where they talked for several hours. Just before they parted, Adams saw the attorney hand Stewart a purple envelope.

Few reports that Adams sent to the Agency during his association with Pinkerton were more important than the one he wrote the next morning. It linked the mysterious lawyer with a man fitting Burns's description of one of the two "undertakers," provided sound evidence that Martin and Stewart were associated in some way and that the lawyer was their means of communication with one another, for, ever since his release, Pinkerton detectives had followed Martin and had noted that he frequently mailed letters in purple envelopes.

Pinkerton's next move was to send John Burns to Toronto. It was rather difficult to transform the toil-worn laborer into a hearty man-about-town, but Adams, a fashionable tailor and an assortment of flashy jewelry accomplished it. When Adams was sure his pupil had learned to conduct himself properly, he took Burns to the gambling house. He behaved beautifully, mingling with the wealthy patrons as if he had never known any other life. Night after night, Burns and Adams visited the tables, until

Burns saw Stewart one evening and whispered to his companion, "There's one of the men I told Mr. Pinkerton about."

Taken to Hamilton, Burns was given several chances to see Martin, but he insisted, "I never saw him before." However, a few days later, in the gaming rooms, he did see somebody he recognized—a handsome man in his middle thirties who sported a trim black mustache. "He's the other one I saw in the Bronx," Burns informed Adams.

Inquiries revealed that the second man was Charles Burnette—to Allan Pinkerton this was obviously an alias for Charles Barret. He also held a long conference with Martin's lawyer. About midnight, the two men were joined by Stewart and then, two hours later, Martin appeared. Although Pinkerton operatives waited outside the gambling rooms to follow them, only Stewart and the lawyer left the building. The others apparently were spending the night with the owner. Unfortunately, the operatives were unable to trail Stewart and the attorney, as they jumped into a carriage and drove quickly away.

The next evening, the lawyer apologized to Adams for ignoring him the previous night. "I didn't mean to be rude," he explained, "but I was quite busy. Two of my clients, Stewart and Burnette—both of New York City—took over this place last night."

"Is that so? It must have cost them a fortune," Adams commented.

"They have the money. They made a killing in New York last May," the lawyer informed him.

Meanwhile, other Pinkerton men were checking the registers of every Toronto hotel. In one they found that a Mr. Charles Burnette had occupied a suite for five months and had been recently joined by his wife. Mrs. Brelsford, Bangs and Pinkerton loitered in the hotel's lobby and finally the lady sleuth saw Burnette's wife. "I don't care what she calls herself, she's the woman I knew as Mrs. Barret," she told her superiors. Pinkerton and Bangs then trailed the suspect to another hotel where a Mr. and Mrs. Charles Stewart were registered.

Pinkerton took all the evidence that he had gathered to Toronto police headquarters and requested the authorities to arrest the Burnettes and the Stewarts. They agreed and the detective arranged for simultaneous raids on the suites occupied by the couples. He also sent telegrams, asking that Martin be taken into custody in Hamilton and Putnam be picked up in New York City.

Actually, only one raid was necessary in Toronto, as the two couples were having dinner in the Stewart suite when the police arrived. There was no trouble gaining entrance. A burly policeman knocked gently on the door and murmured, "Room Service," and Stewart opened it, expecting to find a waiter with the dinner that he had ordered.

As the officers rushed in, Barret dashed to another room and seized a rifle. Before he could pull the trigger or use the gun as a club, Pinkerton grabbed him and threw his arm around the robber's neck—a wrestling grip he used all his life to subdue dangerous men.

When the prisoners were taken to jail, the suite was searched. Many of the stolen securities were found hidden behind the pictures hung on the walls. While rummaging in a dresser Pinkerton found a knife with two nicks in the blade, which he was sure would match the markings he had discovered on the express car door. Meanwhile, in Hamilton, Martin was confessing to the authorities that he had known the bonds he had offered the bank were stolen and volunteered to turn state's evidence.

Stewart, Barret and Martin were extradited to the United States. While Martin talked freely to the police,

Stewart and Barret remained silent, as did Putnam. However, Pinkerton broke down the former baggagemaster by pointing out the flaw in the story he had told in the hospital. Finally, he confessed, "You're right, Mr. Pinkerton, dead right. It was all a fake. They convinced me that I never would be suspected and I fell for it. Then they double-crossed me and I didn't get a cent. That was bad enough, but they really tried to kill me. I moved my head just in time when Barret swung that iron bar."

Both Stewart and Barret received twenty-year sentences. Neither Martin nor Putnam, who co-operated with the prosecution, was imprisoned. As the trial ended, it seemed as if the Merchants' Union Express Company's loss would total nearly $100,000, as only half of the stolen securities were recovered. However, the forced sale of the restaurant and the opulent furnishings of the gambling casino resulted in making up the difference—something that never would have happened if Allan Pinkerton hadn't known how dull a person's reactions are when rudely awakened from a deep sleep or failed to notice some whittling, a sliver of soap and a piece of brass from an accordion.

> *"From the time of the very first settlers, the taming
> of the frontier had been marked by violence."*
> —Penfield

T HE MERCHANTS' UNION EXPRESS COMPANY case was but
one of hundreds in which Allan Pinkerton displayed
his outstanding ability to direct a complicated campaign
against criminals and furnished proof of his brilliant de-
ductive powers. Over the years, his uncanny genius in
finding and interpreting clues—usually overlooked by others—made Allan the most respected and feared law-enforcement officer in the country. No detective had ever
shown greater skill in using physical evidence than Pinkerton. A battered hat left near the body of a young man
beaten to death led Allan to his murderer; the position of
a desk lamp made possible the conviction of a bank robber.

Although Pinkerton never sought personal publicity, he
was justifiably proud of the coverage newspapers gave to
the work of the Agency—*after a case was closed.* In his

memoirs, he frequently complains that an investigation was made more difficult than it should have been because the newspapers kept the criminals informed of what steps were being taken to apprehend them!

There was also another reason why he did not like to see his name in print. Every time Pinkerton solved a case and it was made public, dozens of individuals would write to him, asking for positions on the Agency staff. Some of these requests were so ridiculous that Allan placed them in what he called "The Lunatic File." One of the most amusing applications was from a middle-aged man who "knew he would make a good detective because he had nothing else to do."

While Pinkerton could laugh at some of the requests he received for jobs, others annoyed him almost as much as the reports of petty swindlers who pretended to be Pinkerton operatives. They would cheat storekeepers and hotels by telling clerks to send their bill to the Pinkerton Agency in Chicago.

As more and more newspaper space was given to the Agency and the exploits of its founder, the number of letters asking for a Pinkerton badge increased. The deluge of applications prompted Allan to write: "There seems to be three things that are the ambition of a great class of people who are either in need of employment or who are dissatisfied with the employment they have. They wish to go on the stage, or become an author, or turn detective. It is about an equal chance which way they will go."

While trapping bank robbers, embezzlers, forgers and swindlers made Pinkerton internationally famous, nothing he or his organization did attracted more attention on both sides of the Atlantic than the part the Agency played in bringing law and order to the West. Lured by tales of gold and lush grazing grounds, adventurous men, unable

Robbery of an express messenger

to settle down after serving in the War Between the States, had trekked westward in hopes of making a fortune. Along with their pistols and blankets, many of them carried the hates and fears that they had acquired on the battlefield. For this reason "Johnny Reb" and "Yank" clashed in mining town and cow camp almost as often as did homesteaders and cattle-barons, honest miners and claim-jumpers, express messengers and train robbers, stage coach drivers and holdup men. The whole frontier was a land of violence and killing where there was no law except that of the six-gun.

Pinkerton's National Detective Agency first became involved in this conflict between honest men and outlaws because of its protection contract with the Adams Express Company. Therefore, in 1866, when the Reno Gang, composed of former bounty jumpers turned cattle thieves, counterfeiters and highwaymen, held up a wood-burning train on the Ohio and Mississippi Railroad a few miles from Seymour, Indiana, and robbed the Adams Express Company safe of $10,000, Pinkerton took up their trail. This holdup has a unique place in the history of lawbreaking. It was the first train robbery in the United States and possibly the first anywhere.

The Renos were led by five brothers, John, Frank, William, Sim and Clint, who swaggered through the streets of Seymour, defying honest citizens, for they knew no lawman would dare to arrest them. Gradually, their gang of cutthroats grew large enough so they could extend their operations. Riding fast and shooting to kill, they galloped across Indiana, Illinois and Missouri and came back to their farm in Seymour with their saddlebags full of other people's money.

By the time Pinkerton arrived in Seymour, the Renos had made another haul, looting the county treasurer's office in Gallatin, Missouri, of $22,065. Everybody, including Pinkerton, knew that the Renos were responsible for the theft, but, ignored by authorities and protected by their friends among the townspeople, they rode in and out of Seymour as carelessly as honest farmers.

Realizing that it would be impossible to arrest the five brothers or any member of their gang in Indiana, because they had terrorized and corrupted the entire state, Pinkerton devised an elaborate scheme to trap the outlaws away from home.

Shortly after Pinkerton's visit to Seymour, that town could boast of three new citizens. One had opened a saloon, which soon became a popular hang-out for the more lawless element, another was a gambler and the third, seemingly the only hard-working man among them, got a job loading freight at the railroad station. It didn't take long for the gambler, who said his name was Phil Oates, to become familiar with John Reno, leader of the gang. This detective's special ability to make friends, as well as his skill in handling a deck of cards, had been the reasons why Pinkerton had sent him to Seymour.

Gambler and outlaw would often stroll through Seymour together, therefore John saw no reason to refuse Oates's invitation to go down to the station and see the west-bound train come in late one afternoon. The two men walked slowly to the depot, found a spot where the glare from the setting sun would not block their view of any passengers that alighted from the train and waited for the whistle that would announce that the locomotive had just rounded the bend a half mile down the tracks.

Except for the Pinkerton operative who was busy getting the handcar of freight ready to load on the incoming train, the station platform was deserted. Just before the train pulled in, eight men suddenly appeared, Reno was

not armed and he was soon surrounded, handcuffed and
taken aboard the train by the sheriff of Daviess County,
"six muscular men from Cincinnati" and Allan Pinkerton.
As Number 29 chugged down the track, the Sheriff
showed John Reno his warrant, but the outlaw paid no
attention. He was too stunned to think of anything except
that he had been taken prisoner in his home town where,
heretofore, by fear and bribery, he had literally "got away
with murder."

Number 29 was not quite out of sight when Frank Reno
heard that his brother had been kidnaped by the law.
Frank hastily gathered the gang together and set out in a
special train to rescue John, but he failed to stop Pinkerton.

Although John Reno was given a long sentence, his
band of desperadoes, under Frank Reno's leadership, rode
"high, wide and handsome" all through the Middle West.
Once they actually looted a bank in a town that was
jammed with people because the semi-annual session of
court was being held.

As they were galloping headlong down the main street,
with bullets flying all about them, the eleven outlaws
rode by the railroad station just as a train arrived. In response to Frank's shouted commands, the gang split into
two groups. One rode their horses out of town, leading
the mounts of those of their comrades who had slid out
of their saddles and seized the train at gunpoint. Under
Frank's direction—and six-shooter—the engineer pulled
the train down the track to where the horsemen were
waiting. The gang then robbed the mail car and all the
passengers. Finally, they uncoupled the locomotive, ran
it up the line a safe distance, smashed its controls and
ordered the conductor, "Don't try to warn any train that's
behind you. It won't do any good to flag 'em down. We're

riding that way and we'll attend to stopping any train that comes along!"

All during the winter of 1868 the Reno gang "continued their lawless way." They took $15,000 from the Harrison County Bank in Magnolia, Iowa, and $11,000 from the courthouse office of the treasurer of Mills County. As fast as they rode, Allan Pinkerton was close behind, and he learned how they always knew where county funds were kept. Michael Rogers, a wealthy and respectable citizen of Council Bluffs, Iowa, was, the detective discovered, not what he appeared to be. A real estate dealer, Rogers would visit a treasurer's office to examine land titles and note the location of the safe and the way it was guarded. Then he would pass this information on to the Renos.

Pinkerton captured Frank Reno and his followers in Council Bluffs and saw them placed in cells. Five days later, on the first day of April, they escaped by digging a hole under the wall of the jail. Although they were in a hurry, the outlaws paused long enough to leave Pinkerton a note. It was written in chalk above the hole and read, "April Fool."

Six weeks later, the Renos committed their most successful train robbery, when they held up a Jefferson, Missouri, and Indianapolis Railroad train near Seymour and netted $96,000 in gold, after throwing the express messenger out of his car and fatally injuring him. Flushed with success, the gang boasted that it planned to hold up an incoming train said to be carrying $100,000 in gold from California. Pinkerton arranged that the Adams Express Company car transporting the precious cargo be shifted to another train. When the bandits ripped open the door of the substituted car, they met a barrage of pistol fire from Pinkerton, his son William, and a posse. The Renos retreated, several of them badly wounded. They were trailed by the Pinkertons and the long-suffering honest citizens of Seymour, who had formed a vigilante committee.

Two of the wounded men were captured, but never stood trial. Masked men broke into the jail and lynched them. By riding day and night, William Pinkerton and other operatives caught up with three more of the Reno gang. They planned to take them back to Seymour on a special train, but it never came and they were forced to use a wagon to carry their prisoners. On the way to Seymour, the wagon was overtaken by vigilantes and the outlaws were snatched from their custodians and given "short shrift and a hempen collar."

While William was galloping after minor members of the Reno outfit, his father corralled five of the most important outlaws in the gang, including Frank Reno, in Windsor, Canada. Pinkerton soon found that capturing the men was one thing, getting them to the United States to stand trial was another. A bitter international dispute over the extradition of Pinkerton's prisoners went on for weeks before President Andrew Jackson's request for them was approved by the Canadian authorities. While waiting for a ruling to be made, Allan had to be constantly alert because frequent attempts to murder him were made by friends of the Renos. One, that nearly succeeded, took place on the ferry that ran between Windsor and Detroit. As the would-be assassin cocked his revolver, Pinkerton lunged at him, tore the gun out of his hand, hit him on the jaw, placed handcuffs on his wrists, then lugged the unconscious man to Detroit police headquarters.

The detective had another narrow escape on the day he finally took his shackled prisoners from the Windsor jail and boarded a hired tug for the trip across the river to Detroit. In midstream, a steamer ploughed into the tug and cut it in two, throwing Pinkerton, his assistants and the Renos into the water. Weighed down by leg irons and handcuffs, the prisoners would have drowned if their captors had not kept them afloat until another boat came to their rescue.

It would have been just as well for the outlaws if they had sunk. While in their cells in the New Albany, Indiana, jail awaiting trial, members of a well-organized mob stormed the building, overpowered the sheriff and his deputies and, with ropes, ended the careers of "the thieves, robbers, murderers and desperadoes, who for many years defied law and order, and threatened the lives and property of honest citizens."

* * *

William Pinkerton and his father were not the only members of the Agency staff who rode "shotgun" on stage-coaches, battled blizzards and sandstorms, slept in the saddle and suffered thirst and hunger while chasing out-laws. Operative Yankee Bligh captured two of Jesse James's gang. Operative Louis Lull was murdered while tracking Jim and John Younger, who had ridden with Jesse in Quantrell's infamous guerrilla band during the War Between the States and had joined his band of des-peradoes. Because of its protection contracts with various express companies, the American Bankers Association and railroads, the Agency employed a large force on the fron-tier. Some of the most famous manhunters that ever led a posse were Pinkerton operatives. Among them were Tom Horn, Charles Siringo and William Minster. The latter has the distinction of having arrested Bill Miner, the bandit legend claims was the first man to say "Hands up," when staging a robbery.

Over the years, the words "Hands up" have played an

important part in publicizing the work of the Pinkertons. Formerly, a poster depicting a masked highwayman with a drawn gun that seemed to point at the viewer's eyes, irrespective of the angle from which it was viewed, was distributed for advertising purposes. Moreover, it was the habit of William and Robert Pinkerton to give as Christmas gifts various articles of sterling silver, such as ashtrays, cigarette boxes and letter openers—on which were embossed the figure of a masked highwayman with his gun pointed in all directions simultaneously and the words "Hands up."

Both the gifts and the poster originated from an oil painting which hung in the "Owl," a famous café in Spokane, Washington, in 1888. Painted by a colorful character of the Old West, known as "The Cowboy Artist," the picture was of particular interest to the Pinkertons because of its history.

"The Cowboy Artist" happened to be in Reno, Nevada, when a stranger in that wild and lawless town was tried on the charge of being the masked bandit who specialized in robbing gambling houses. His victims reported that he would rush in, shout "Hands up!" and cover both players and employees with his pistol. Evidence against the stranger was more than enough to convince the jury of miners. He had a gun similar to the one used by the bandit, gold coins in his pocket and no good excuse for being in Reno.

A dozen witnesses, all known for their ability to draw fast and shoot straight, identified the prisoner as the masked highwayman. Asked by the defense attorney why they didn't attempt to shoot it out with his client, each claimed that the bandit was pointing his gun and looking directly at him all the time! The lawyer immediately pointed out that one man couldn't look "square at a dozen people at the same time," and therefore, only one of the

All previous reward circulars issued by this Agency, referring to this robbery are annulled.

ROB'T A. PINKERTON, Gen'l. Sup't.
EASTERN DIVISION,
NEW YORK.

WM. A. PINKERTON, Gen'l. Sup't.
WESTERN DIVISION,
CHICAGO, ILL'S.

WE NEVER SLEEP

PINKERTON'S NATIONAL DETECTIVE AGENCY
FOUNDED BY ALLAN PINKERTON, 1850.

CHICAGO:
192 & 193 FIFTH AVENUE
WM. A. PINKERTON, Sup't

PHILADELPHIA:
45 SOUTH THIRD STREET.
R. J. LINDEN. Sup't

NEW YORK:
66 EXCHANGE PLACE,
GEO. D. BANGS, Sup't.

BOSTON:
42 & 44 COURT STREET,
JOHN CORNISH, Sup't.

ST. PAUL:
63 TO 66 UNION BLOCK,
W. J. LOADER. Sup't.

DENVER:
1 & 2 OPERA HOUSE BLOCK
CHAS. O. EAMES, Sup't

ATTORNEYS FOR THE AGENCY.
CLARENCE A. SEWARD, NEW YORK.   LEWIS C. CASSIDY, PHILADELPHIA.

$700 REWARD.

REUBEN HOUSTON BURROWS, alias **RUBE BURROWS**, charged with highway robbery, having, with his brother, **JAMES BUCHANAN BURROWS, and others**, wearing masks on the night of **FRIDAY, DECEMBER 9, 1887**, boarded the north bound train on the St. Louis, Arkansas & Texas R. R. at Genoa Station, Ark., and compelled the messenger of the **SOUTHERN EXPRESS COMPANY** to surrender the keys of his safe, which they rifled of $3,500. **James Buchanan Burrows**, and three others of the robbers, **have since been arrested.**

In an attempt to arrest **Reuben Burrows and Jim Burrows in Montgomery, Alabama**, on January 23, 1888, **Reuben Burrows** shot Mr. Neil Bray, a compositor on the *Advertiser*, who had been called on and was aiding the officer in his arrest.

DESCRIPTION.

REUBEN HOUSTON BURROWS is about 32 years of age, 6 feet in height, weighs about 160 pounds, blue eyes which do not look a person full in the face, round head, wears 7¼ hat, full forehead, face broad under the ears but thin near the mouth, short, inclined to pug-shaped nose, swarthy or sandy complexion, light sandy hair, thin light moustache, uses Hair Vigor to darken hair; left arm is a little shorter than the right, caused by having been broken at bend of arm; rather a lounging gait, carrying his hands in his pockets in a leisurely way.

Usually wears dark clothes and woolen shirts, a No. 8 boot, but no jewelry. Does not use tobacco; drinks, but not to excess; does not gamble, but can play the game of seven-up; is somewhat of a country story teller, relating stories of snake, dog and cat fights, etc. Is a good horseman, carries a 45-calibre pistol and is a good shot.

He was born in Lamar county, Alabama, is married, and has two children who are now with his father in Alabama. His wife is residing with her father, Mr. Hoover, at Alexandria, Alabama. He resided for 14 years in Wise and Erath counties, Texas; has worked for the Mexican Central R. R., and is a member of the Masonic fraternity.

The **Southern Express Company**, and the **St. Louis, Arkansas and Texas Railroad Co.** have jointly offered a **reward of Five Hundred Dollars ($500)**, and in addition the Governor of the State of Arkansas has offered a **reward of Two Hundred Dollars ($200)** for the arrest, delivery to the authorities of the State of Arkansas, and conviction of **Reuben Houston Burrows.**

Send information to

Or to any Superintendent of

Pinkerton's National Detective Agency,
At Either of the Above Listed Offices.

WM. A. PINKERTON, General Superintendent Western Division, Chicago, Ill.

C. T. CAMPBELL,
Sup't Texas Express,
TEXARKANA, ARK.

Chicago, February 20, 1888.

Reward circular of the Pinkerton's National Detective Agency witnesses could be telling the truth. As a result, the stranger was freed.

As "The Cowboy Artist" sat listening to this legal argument he was inspired to paint a picture of a masked highwayman with a drawn pistol that gave the optical illusion of being pointed in all directions at once. His portrait, for which an old scout and trapper was the model, particularly interested the Pinkertons because the suspect who had been tried in Reno was one of their operatives, working undercover on a railroad wrecking case, and he could not reveal his identity!

However, "The Pinks" did tear the mask off the real masked highwayman shortly afterwards. Operatives working for the Jewelers' Protective Union, in Colorado, took the bandit into custody for holding up and robbing a jewelry salesman, and he was sentenced to twenty years.

The operative in the masked highwayman incident was not the only Pinkerton agent who was accused of being a criminal. Because they would no longer be able to serve as undercover agents if they showed their credentials, operatives often were jailed. If their sentence was a short one, they never revealed their true identity, feeling that a jail term would make their disguises more effective. However, if an operative was falsely charged with a major crime, the Agency secretly informed the authorities and he was released—usually by "escaping."

One of the most brilliant undercover assignments of any Pinkerton range detective was carried out by Charles Siringo, who could track an outlaw band with the skill of an Indian scout. Under William Pinkerton's direction, Siringo loped into Powder Springs, Colorado, where Butch Cassidy, whom the Pinkertons were later to chase through the jungles of South America, had organized the Train Robbers' Syndicate. Composed of cowboys and outlaws, the outfit had been formed to prey upon railroads and express companies.

When Siringo reached Cassidy's headquarters, he dismounted, tied his pinto to a hitching-rack, flicked the dust off his Stetson and loosened his Colts in their holsters. He was immediately accepted as a gunman from Texas, but the syndicate never found out how fast he could draw. Every time they planned to rob a train, the railroad schedule was changed. Eventually, Cassidy realized where the leak was, but when he went gunning for the "Texan," he was gone.

William Pinkerton undertook as many dangerous assignments in the cattle and mining country as any of his father's assistants did. Accompanied by his brother or other operatives or at times, working alone, Billy rode fearlessly after such famous "badmen" as Sam Bass, train robber and road agent; the Dalton boys, who started out as peace officers and ended by robbing and murdering their way across Oklahoma; the Sontag brothers who frequently stopped stagecoaches to see "if there are any Pinkertons aboard that we can kill"; and many others.

The Sontags were not the only outlaws that swore to kill everyone who wore a Pinkerton badge. The Younger brothers, the Farringtons and the Renos had also done so, but none of them hated Allan Pinkerton as much as Jesse James did.

Missouri-born Jesse had been well-educated in the arts of arson, murder and pillage. His instructor was William Clarke Quantrell, a one-time schoolteacher who pretended to support the South by confining his plundering and murders to free soil. Jesse was not quite sixteen when, as one of Quantrell's guerrillas, he rode into Lawrence, Kansas, an anti-slavery stronghold, on August 13, 1863. Quantrell had ordered that every male citizen of the town be killed and all its buildings burned. His men failed to carry out his command, but when the last blood-chilling "*Yip-yip-ya-aw-aw!*" of the raiders died away, over a hundred lay dead on the streets of Lawrence and nearly two hundred buildings were smoking ruins. A year later, Jesse killed his share of unarmed Union soldiers on a hospital train and, in the afternoon of the same day, he played an important part in the ambush of Federal troops.

When the war was over, most of Quantrell's men hung up their guns, sick of bloodshed. However, Jesse, his brother Frank, their good friends and neighbors the Youngers and some others chose to live by the gun. Before long, Jesse and his companions were preying upon Pinkerton clients and the Agency began hounding them. Strangely, Jesse spied on the detectives twice while they were looking for him. Curious as to what Allan and Robert looked like, he let his hair grow, bought some "store clothes," went to Chicago and got a good look at them when they came out of the building in which their office was located. Several years later, furious at Pinkerton's success in capturing some of his band, Jesse again went to Chicago—not to look at Allan, but to kill him. He changed his mind at the last minute because "to shoot him down would be too swift . . . I want him to feel it."

Beside outlaws who had ridden with Quantrell, "the bloodiest man in American history," the Pinkertons matched wits and traded bullets with cowboys who had taken "the hoot-owl trail." Most of them were young men who were unable to get jobs herding cattle because so many ranchers went bankrupt during the long drought of the 1870's. Some became famous bandits, others met a bullet from a peace officer's gun and were buried in an unmarked grave.

Before train robbery became profitable, stagecoaches

were the main prey of these desperadoes. No one knows how many coaches were held up over the years. In 1900, William Pinkerton, speaking before the Police Chiefs Association, declared that he had no idea how many road agents his operatives had arrested for this crime. Incidentally, the last recorded stagecoach robbery was committed by an attractive young woman in Globe, Arizona, in 1909.

Not as pretty as Pearl Hart, who held up the Globe stage, but far more colorful was Charles Bolton, known to the Pinkertons and "knights of the road" alike as Black Bart. After every holdup, Bart would leave behind a bit of poorly written verse signed "Black Bart, PO-8."

Pretty, poetical or plain evil, no matter how fast their draw, how remote their hide-out, outlaws from the Middle Border to California learned to fear the men who wore the Pinkerton badge. Safe in their comfortable homes in the cities of the East, newspaper readers eagerly read about the brave exploits of "The Pinks" in their pursuit of notorious outlaws. As a result, the Agency's reputation grew and its operatives' exploits excited the imagination of the public.

16

*". . . coal cars down from Scranton, piled with
anthracite like jet."*

—Hoffman

WITH WILLIAM AND ROBERT working in the New York
and Chicago offices of the Agency and proving
they were capable of handling any type of investigation,
Allan, who was not too well and very tired, spent more
and more time on his model farm near Onorga, Illinois.
Pinkerton was extremely fond of horses in general and of
his own thoroughbred stock in particular. His sons inherited his appreciation of horseflesh and would, in time,
play an important part in driving crooked gamblers, dishonest jockeys and unsavory characters from American
race tracks.

When not at Onorga, the senior Pinkerton relaxed by
writing his memoirs. Unfortunately, the frightful Chicago
Fire of 1871—the worst disaster that had as yet befallen
an American city—had destroyed most of his records. Nevertheless, the master sleuth's marvelous memory enabled

him to recall enough material to fill eighteen books, some
containing seven hundred pages of closely printed type.
Their titles reflect his wide and varied career:

Gypsies and Detectives
A Double Life and Detectives
Bucholz and Detectives
The Spiritualists and Detectives
The Mississippi Outlaws and Detectives
Strikers, Communists, and Detectives
The Spy of the Rebellion
Bank Robbers and Detectives
The Railroad Forger and Detectives
Criminal Reminiscences and Detectives
The Expressmen and Detectives
The Mollie Maguires and Detectives
Professional Thieves and Detectives
Thirty Years a Detective
The Model Town and Detectives
The Somnambulist and Detectives
Claude Melnotte as a Detective
The Burglar's Fate and Detectives

Judged by present-day standards, Pinkerton overwrote
and his style might be considered flowery. However, no
modern author describes people with more skill than Allan
showed in his word portraits of honest men and criminals.
Long out of print—although a special edition of all his
books was issued the year of his death—Allan Pinkerton's
volumes, with their dated but fascinating illustrations, are
still exciting reading. They are not only crammed with
high adventure, but also provide a graphic picture of life
in the United States during an important formative period.

Like all authors, Pinkerton was proud of his books, yet

over and over again, in the preface he wrote for each one, Allan explains that he wrote them "in the hope that I may, while interesting my readers in the romance of detective operations, point out to all the enduring moral of strict integrity and honorable conduct."

While Pinkerton the detective was modest about his achievements, Pinkerton the author would boast now and then about the Agency and write: "Our triumph in bringing to justice the bold criminals depicted in this work only differs in circumstances from scores of successes that we have achieved from time to time." At the same time, Allan would frankly admit that in certain cases "our theories and conclusions were at fault."

Long before television announcers began informing their viewers that "the facts you have heard are true, only the names have been changed to protect the innocent," Pinkerton was saying the same thing: "The stories as related by me are essentially true; the incidents depicted have occurred, and the people of whom I treat, were, and many of them are, living men and women. It is only in the locality of the scenes enacted, and in the names, which I have given to the actors in these criminal dramas, that a variance with truth may be successfully alleged. In thus concealing the identity of those, whose crimes have brought them under the penalties of the law, I have been actuated by a sincere desire for their eventual reformation, and I have, therefore, withheld their real names, in order that no undue obstacles to that much desired reformation should be placed in their way."

Allan Pinkerton, the real detective, clashed with Sir Arthur Conan Doyle, creator of the most famous detective of fiction, Sherlock Holmes, over one of his books. Allan sued Sir Arthur, claiming that he had obtained the plot for his *The Valley of Fear* from Pinkerton's *The Mollie Maguires and Detectives.*

The latter title tells the story of one of the most famous investigations ever conducted by the Agency. It began in October, 1873, when Franklin B. Gowen of the Philadelphia and Reading Railroad asked Pinkerton to come to his office. Gowen told the detective that a secret society had been formed in the Pennsylvania coal fields by the miners and that they were defying the law, brutally beating or murdering all who opposed them. Originally, Gowen explained, the organization, modeled after one formed in Ireland to intimidate absentee landlords and prevent tenant farmers from being evicted, strove to improve working conditions and secure higher wages. However, by degrees, a lawless element took over the Mollie Maguires —so-called because the group in Ireland had worn women's clothes as a disguise when hiding from the police— and now they terrorized the hard-coal counties of eastern Pennsylvania.

"It is impossible to do anything about the Mollies, Pinkerton," Gowen continued. "They control the local police and they take no chances, even though they are lawless men. For example, when they decide to murder somebody, a member of the organization from another district is brought in so that he won't be recognized. Frankly, between their activities and business conditions, my railroad and many mine owners are losing money. I know you can't do anything about business conditions, but do you think you can do something about the Mollie Maguires?"

Pinkerton thought he could. In order to wipe out the Mollies, he would have to gather evidence of their crimes that would stand up in court. After thinking the problem over, he decided that the only way this could be done was

to send an undercover operative into the coal fields with
orders to spy upon the Mollies.

"What we need," Allan told Bangs, "is a man with special qualifications. He must be brave, strong and Irish.
Whom do you suggest?"

Bangs could not think of any operative who could undertake the mission, nor could Pinkerton. Then, after the
latter's return to Chicago, he happened to see one of his
detectives that he had completely forgotten about working as a conductor on a horsecar. This man's assignment
was to help stop petty pilfering, for, although the transit
line carried thousands of passengers every day, only hundreds of fares were turned in by its employees. As Pinkerton looked at twenty-nine-year-old James McParland,
who was Irish-born, had a keen mind and a friendly personality, he knew that he had found the operative to send
to the coal mines. Beyond all doubt, this is the outstanding example of Pinkerton's uncanny genius for picking the
right man for an investigation. James McParland was to
perform what many criminologists have called "the greatest feat in detective history."

McParland was relieved from his transit company assignment and told to report to the Agency office. As soon
as he arrived, he was directed to his chief's private room
and the door was carefully closed. Allan wasted no words.
He bluntly outlined what was happening in Pennsylvania
and told of his promise to Gowen. "Now, remember, you
don't have to take this assignment," he assured McParland. "I'll never question your courage if you refuse. It
may be that sending a man after the Mollie Maguires is
the same as sending him to certain death. The choice is
up to you."

"May I ask a few questions?" McParland inquired. After
listening to his superior's replies, the operative said, "I'll

go to Pennsylvania whenever you like, Major. Just what
do you want me to do?"

"What I want sounds easy to get, but, believe me, I
know that it isn't. I want evidence that will stamp out the
Mollie Maguires and put the men responsible for the murders, stabbings and beatings I've told you about behind
bars."

"I'll do my best, sir," promised McParland. "Have you
any suggestions?"

"First, remember that no one, not even your fellow operatives, are to know that you are investigating the Mollie
Maguires. This case must be handled secretly. We can't
take the chance of having it known that the Agency has
even been engaged to wipe out the Mollies—it would
mean your death. You'll be in danger enough, for the only
way I can see by which you might gather the evidence we
want is through joining the Maguires and so learning their
plans. Remember, you must look, act and talk like a coal
miner all the time—one slip and you'll forfeit your life.
That's all I can tell you, McParland, except that, before
you leave, you'd best get some suitable clothes."

McParland got his "suitable clothes" from the Agency's
well-stocked wardrobe. They consisted of well-worn,
down-at-the-heel hobnailed boots, roughly patched pants,
a threadbare shirt, a tattered jacket and a filthy shapeless
hat. However, when he reported at the Agency office the
next morning, he was dressed in a well-tailored suit and
carried a brand-new suitcase.

His appearance set off a series of facetious jibes from
the other operatives, who asked if he were getting married, had inherited a fortune or was trying to look like a
gentleman. McParland's nimble wit had an answer for all
their sallies and, when one man demanded, "Taking a trip,
Jimmy? Where are you going? To Europe?" his reply clev-

erly explained why his associates would not see him for
some time.

"As a matter of fact, I am," he responded gaily. "The
Major is sending me to England to wind up that counterfeiting case. While I'm overseas, I'm taking a little vacation and visiting my relatives in Ireland. I just came in to
say good-by to you boys. I'll see you when I get back—
that is, if I do come back. They may offer me the chief
inspector's job at Scotland Yard and, much as I'd miss you
all, I'd have to accept. 'Twould be bad manners to refuse
the offer!"

Waving his hand in response to the jeers that greeted
this statement, McParland began his trip. However, instead of going to England, he went to Philadelphia. Pinkerton had arranged for McParland to meet secretly Superintendent Franklin, head of the newly opened Agency
office in that city, as soon as he arrived. Franklin, who had
held several conferences with Gowen and other officials
of railroads serving the coal fields and mine owners, gave
the Chicago operative the latest information about the
criminal activities of the Mollie Maguires. The two men
also arranged a code for McParland to use when sending
reports. The Superintendent promised to keep the young
detective supplied with stamps, because uneducated
miners were apt to become suspicious of one of their number who wrote so many letters that he constantly needed
to buy stamps at the post office.

After talking with Franklin, McParland put on his rag-
ged clothing, discarded his razor and began to perfect
his disguise. He spent a week on the coal docks, talking
with laborers, memorizing their expressions and observing
their ways. Then, overnight, James McParland vanished.
But the next day one James McKenna, toting two battered
suitcases, boarded a Philadelphia & Reading train with a

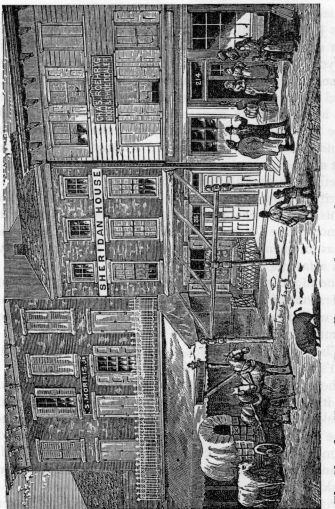

The Sheridan House in Pottsville, Pennsylvania, where Detective McParlan became friendly with leaders of the Molly Maguires

ticket for Port Clinton tucked in the grimy sweatband of his hat.

As James McKenna, the Pinkerton operative wandered from one mining town to another, making friends with everyone he met. Yet, although he listened to the talk in saloons, on street corners and in poolrooms, McParland heard nothing that was worth reporting to Franklin. He did, however, learn something that was to be of great value to himself. Idling in a tavern in the small town of Tremont one night, he overheard a miner give a strange toast and he memorized it because of a feeling that it had something to do with the Maguires.

Drifting from town to town, McParland gradually built up his assumed character. Before long, he was known in Tremont, Pine Grove, Middle Creek and other communities as an unemployed miner who could liven up a party with a fast jig or sentimental song.

One night, after he had entertained a rowdy group of miners, one of them suggested to McKenna that he might find work in either Tamaqua or Mahanoy City because the mines in those towns were very busy.

"Then too," Nick Brennan informed his companion, "that's the ground where the boys are true!"

The minute he heard these words, McParland realized that it was a password of some kind and that Brennan had mistaken him for a member of the Mollie Maguires. Because he had no idea of the correct response, he poured Brennan another drink, clapped him on the back and said, "Thanks for the tip. I could use some work. Tell me, who should I see when I get there?"

Brennan gave the operative the names and addresses of "some good boys," but McParland, feeling that his new-found friend might be testing him, did not go directly to Mahanoy City, but continued tramping about the countryside. In Tower City, he was warned by a well-meaning acquaintance to stay away from Pat Dormer's saloon because it was the local headquarters of the Maguires. As soon as he could, the detective went to Dormer's establishment. Within a week he was considered a regular patron and was always welcomed by other customers because of his willingness to treat, the way he danced and his ballad singing. Dormer also liked the "grand boy, Mc-Kenna." Not only did he attract trade, but he told the tavern keeper exciting stories of his adventures in the Colorado mining country when business was slack.

One night, after singing and dancing, "McKenna" was invited to join a game of euchre in the back room. After a few minutes of play, the detective's Pinkerton training enabled him to catch the dealer cheating and he exposed him. The cheat heatedly denied the charge and challenged McParland to a fight. Chairs were pushed back, tables set against the wall and a ring marked off. With Dormer as his second, the operative engaged in a bare-knuckle slugging match with the cardsharp. Although no match for his opponent in weight, reach or size, McParland was a trained boxer and in a few minutes his adversary dropped senseless to the floor, severely beaten.

As the onlookers' cheers died down, the detective walked over to the bar, pounded on it with both fists, then raised a drink high in the air and cried, "Here's to the power that makes English landlords tremble! Here's confusion to all the enemies of old Ireland!"

A sudden hush fell over the room as McParland repeated the toast he had heard in Tremont. Then, a hubbub arose and Dormer, bending close to the detective's ear, whispered in a hoarse voice, "Boy, do you belong?"

"That I did in the old country and would again," McParland replied. Then, realizing that he might not have the proper answer to the next question, he pretended to be overcome by exhaustion and liquor and acted as if he were drunk.

A few days later, Dormer suggested that "McKenna" go to Shenandoah and see Mike Lawler, the bodymaster of the local branch of the Maguires, and ask him for help in finding work. McParland agreed that it was a good idea, but, wary of a trap, he resumed his wanderings before introducing himself as a friend of Dormer's to the leader of the Mollie Maguire lodge in Shenandoah.

"Muff" Lawler read the letter Dormer had written and welcomed McParland. Making friends in Shenandoah proved no more difficult to the jigging and singing "McKenna" than it had in other coal towns. Before long, he was known and liked by many of the local Mollie Maguires, who respected his ability with his fists, enjoyed his tall tales of mining in Colorado and envied him because, although he claimed that he hadn't worked in months, there was always enough money in his pockets to play cards or to buy a friend a drink—Agency rules had long since been discarded.

In order to allay any suspicions as to why he could spend money so freely without any sign of having done an honest—or dishonest—day's work since leaving Colorado, the operative let it be known that, from time to time, he peddled counterfeit money. "Besides," he admitted to Lawler, "though I'm against the government, I'd be a fool to refuse the pension they gave me for my work in the Navy during the war."

Not only was Lawler convinced that this story was true, but he spread it all over town—just as McParland had hoped he would do—and everybody believed it. As the weeks passed, Lawler, like Dormer, became quite fond of the "grand boy, McKenna" and, early in February,

1874, he asked the detective if he would like to board in his house. This offer was instantly accepted. McParland soon found that one of the main advantages of living in the Lawler household was the fact that Mrs. Lawler was an excellent laundress and used blueing in her wash. This made a good substitute for ink and McParland used it to write daily reports to Superintendent Franklin in Philadelphia.

Once in a while, when the blueing bottle was empty, McParland scraped soot from the fireplace, mixed it with water and used it as ink. As a result, his reports were covered with blots and stains, but they always arrived on time. The mailing of these reports was one of the most difficult and risky aspects of McParland's masquerade. Not daring to be seen going to the post office, the operative would wait until late at night "and, by the illumination granted by the stars alone, wend his way to the post office where he would deposit his parcel in the outside box and no person would be the wiser."

Fortunately, Franklin kept him supplied with stamps, as promised. The only problem was where to hide them. Anyone searching his suitcases—he deliberately kept them unlocked to show he had nothing to hide—would not question the package of inexpensive paper and envelopes stored there, but a large supply of stamps was sure to excite suspicion. Therefore, he cut a slit in the sheepskin lining of one of his boots—he had only a single pair—and carried them everywhere he went.

When McParland moved to Lawler's house, the bodymaster of the Shenandoah lodge promised his boarder two things. He would get him a job in the mines and arrange for his reinitiation into the Mollie Maguires. Despite the fact that men were being laid off, Lawler kept the first part of his promise almost immediately. The operative went to work as a laborer, loading coal into the wagons that emptied into the breaker. His job was to shovel twenty tons of anthracite a day. It was back-breaking work and long before McParland's initial shift was over —his hours were from six in the morning until half-past five at night—he was ready to quit. However, the operative knew that, if he threw down his shovel, no one would ever believe that he had worked in the mines in Colorado, so he kept on shoveling. That night, his fingers were so raw that he could hardly hold his knife and fork at the supper table.

By degrees, McParland became used to the physical demands of his job and was able to resume mingling with his friends among the Mollie Maguires after work. As he talked to them, the detective learned of beatings, sabotage and murders and he relayed each piece of information to Franklin. Then he caught his hand between two car wheels and was unable to write—which, in some ways, made no difference to his superiors, as his ink made from blueing or soot often made reading his reports impossible. Shortly after being transferred to an easier job because of his injured hand, McParland was laid off because there was little demand for coal and the mines were closing down.

When Pinkerton heard this, he advised his agent to resume his wanderings. McParland told Lawler that he had a chance to pass some counterfeit money and had made up his mind to leave town.

"Don't do it, Jimmy; don't do it," Lawler begged. "The boys all like you and, with the election coming up, you can be a big help to me. Frank McAndrew wants to be bodymaster and it might be he could get it. I can use you, Jimmy boy. Tell you what I'll do. Stay in Shenandoah and help me with the election and I'll get you in the lodge at the next meeting."

"Jimmy boy" agreed and two weeks later he was initiated into the Mollie Maguires. At the ceremony, he learned the secret signs, symbols, passwords and toasts—all of which he passed on to Franklin in a report written that night by the light of a flickering miner's lamp.

Although most of the mines were shutting down, the Mollie Maguires in Shenandoah were more interested in the election of a bodymaster than in their chances of being unemployed. Somehow, McParland managed to remain friends with everyone in the lodge, despite the contested election. As a result, not even Lawler was surprised when, after his rival, Frank McAndrew, was elected bodymaster, the new chief appointed the "grand boy, McKenna" as secretary. McAndrew had two reasons for choosing the new secretary—he liked Jimmy and, what was more, he could write!

As secretary of the local lodge, McParland was in an ideal position to learn all the secrets of the body and to copy its records. Not only did his ability to write—which was very rare in Shenandoah—enable him to send valuable information to the Agency, it also made him extremely popular with the girls. This was because he wrote their love letters for them.

McParland was admired by the gambling crowd as well. They envied his skill in training Lawler's fighting cocks, his ability to pick winners in dog fights and his professional boxing style. Before long, a great many Mollies in Shenandoah began a campaign to elect him bodymaster of the lodge when McAndrew's term of office was over.

While this compliment convinced McParland that even the most suspicious member of the organization accepted him as a rough, wandering miner, the detective was actually afraid that the Mollies might throw McAndrew out and elect him bodymaster. Conditions in the coal fields had grown steadily worse and work had become increasingly hard to find. The Mollies had let it be known that they intended to keep any available jobs for their membership, even if they had to kill other miners in order to get them. The detective knew that, if he were made bodymaster, in all probability, he would have to plot and carry out assassinations.

As dissatisfaction with McAndrew spread through the lodge, McParland, brave as he was, wished he had never agreed to undertake his assignment. There was no doubt that the Mollies were going to hold a special election and make him bodymaster. McParland didn't know what to do. If he refused the office, all his acting of the past nine months would be wasted. If he accepted, he might have to kill in order to prove he was a loyal Mollie.

There was only one way out. McParland began to drink more and more, hoping to give the impression that he could not be trusted to handle any important work for the Mollies because he was a drunkard. As a result, cheap whiskey ruined his health. While confined to bed, all his hair fell out and, upon recovering, he was forced to buy a wig. It was a far more brilliant red than his own hair had been and, since it was never combed, gave the detective a startling appearance. Moreover, his constant brawling—which was done deliberately—gave him such an unsavory reputation, even in the dives frequented by miners, that he was not allowed to enter them.

Shortly before Christmas, the mines were practically shut down, but the Mollies, anxious to show their power called a strike. Most of the miners who were fortunate enough to be working wanted to stay on the job—and there were hundreds of others anxious to take their places. Nev-

ertheless, the Mollies posted armed guards at the mouth
of each shaft, to prevent anyone from working. Miners
who attempted to enter the mines or who even protested
were beaten, their houses were burned and, in some cases,
those who defied the gang were murdered. In one day, six
men were killed for refusing to obey the Mollies' strike
order.

Although his physical condition had deteriorated terribly, McParland's mind was as alert as it was the day he
left Chicago. Whenever he heard of plans to torture or kill
a miner, he did his best to send the man a warning, while,
at the same time, he pretended to support the strike. Each
night, he sent his report to Franklin and carefully recorded the names of every individual who had, as a member of the Mollies, committed a crime to prolong the
strike. Some nights he listed as many as a dozen names—
the organization was blowing up mines, wrecking trains
and looting stores, as well as engaging in murder and arson.

In April, 1875, after telling his friends in Shenandoah
that he was going to his sister's wedding—later, he gave
them a colorful account of the affair that never took place
—McParland went to Philadelphia. At a meeting with Pinkerton, Franklin and Gowen, the detective summarized
what had happened during his months in the coal fields.
After hearing how serious the situation was, the group decided that more Pinkerton agents should be sent to mining
towns. Unlike McParland, they were to act openly as
members of the Coal and Iron Police, a force recruited by
the mine operators to protect their interests.

The Pinkerton operatives, under the direction of Captain Robert Linden of the Chicago office of the Agency,
reached Shenandoah shortly afterwards. As arranged,
Linden and McParland met "accidentally" in a disreputa-

ble resort frequented by the Mollies, so that the undercover operative could point out to the newcomer the men
he would have to arrest.

When Linden entered the room, he stuck out his hand
and cried, "Jimmy McKenna! I haven't laid eyes on you
since the old days in Buffalo!"

"In spite of what you are and what you do," replied
McParland, "I'll take your hand for old times' sake."

"Oh, stop that talk, Jim. We're old friends. Do you think
I'd trouble you or any of your friends? Come on, everybody, up to the bar. I'm buying a round."

If Linden's remarks to his old friend didn't convince
bystanders that no Mollie had anything to fear from "The
Pinks," his invitation did. Moreover, it established the fact
that McKenna and Linden had known each other for
years. This made it possible for the two men to stop and
talk whenever they met on the street. When they did, under the cover of what appeared to be idle conversation,
the two detectives exchanged information, and, when
they shook hands, McParland slipped tightly folded notes
to Linden, instead of writing lengthy reports.

Meanwhile, the Mollies, feeling more secure than ever
because of their belief that their associate and the Pinkerton man were good friends, continued their ruthless actions. McParland, the Coal and Iron Police and the few
honest lawmen in the coal towns were powerless against
their reign of terror. However, the file of evidence against
the Mollie Maguires grew thicker and thicker. Then, at
long last, honest citizens rebelled and boldly talked of
their plans to form a vigilance committee to drive the
murderers out of the state—and high on the list of the men
they planned to punish was the notorious James Mc-
Kenna.

Before this hotheaded talk gave way to action, two

members of the Mollies and the bodymaster of the Tamaqua lodge were indicted for a murder on the basis of evidence furnished the authorities by McParland. Kerrigan, the bodymaster, decided to turn state's evidence. While the Mollies were reeling from this blow, they suffered a more severe one. A list of members of the organization, arranged by counties, painstakingly compiled by McParland, was distributed to the newspapers by Pinkerton. This meant but one thing—and every member of the Mollie Maguires shuddered at the thought—there was a spy in their ranks!

The spy was a very sick man. Worn out physically and mentally, almost blind and in serious danger of being unmasked, McParland asked Franklin to have him arrested. Being in jail would serve two purposes. It would give the undercover operative a chance to get the medical attention he so sorely needed and, at the same time, would provide additional proof that he was one of the "true boys." However, before his arrest could be arranged, rumors that McKenna was actually a Pinkerton agent spread through the brotherhood.

McAndrew, always a loyal friend of the "grand boy, McKenna," told him of his danger. He also informed the detective that he had prevented several attempts to murder him. Instead of leaving town, McParland went to the men who were accusing him of being a spy and demanded that they prove their charges. They promised to call a special meeting of the leaders of the Maguires so that he could defend himself, but McParland realized that they were planning to kill him. No matter where he went, he was followed by armed men, but he continued to defy anyone to prove that he was a detective. McParland's bluster and bluff worked, although he narrowly missed death on several occasions, but, finally, he decided that his acting would not save his life. Hitching a ride on a sleigh, he told the driver he had to get to the station in a hurry to catch a train because he had just received word that his sister was dying. In this way, he outwitted his would-be assassins.

They arrived at the station just as James McParland, alias James McKenna, rode away to safety and an honored place in the history of law enforcement.

* * *

Although it had been understood that McParland would not have to go to court and testify when any members of the Mollie Maguires were brought to trial, Gowen asked him to do so. Gowen pointed out that his testimony would be invaluable and McParland agreed, despite his poor physical condition, but insisted that he be summoned to court as a detective. McParland also demanded that no bodyguards accompany him when he returned to the coal fields. Gowen readily consented to McParland's first stipulation, but Pinkerton paid absolutely no attention to the second. Operatives Gilchrist and Deacon, the two outstanding marksmen on the Agency payroll, remained on either side of McParland during the entire courtroom proceedings, much to his disgust.

The defense lawyers—the Mollies had raised $30,000 to pay their fees and to hire assassins to murder McParland and Linden—could do little against the mass of evidence in Pinkerton's files. Their only hope was to convince the jury that no crime had been committed by a member of the Mollie Maguires until after McParland came to the coal fields. He had, they claimed, been hired by the mine owners to stir up trouble so that the Coal and Iron police force could intimidate honest men who only wanted better working conditions and higher pay. This ingenious argument failed to impress anyone when Gowen, who was acting as one of the prosecuting lawyers, recited the long list of crimes that had taken place in the mining districts before he had asked Pinkerton's National Detective Agency to investigate the activities of the Mollie Maguires. Wholesale verdicts of "guilty" followed his testimony.

As usual, newspapers were full of praise for the way Pinkerton had brought law and order to the coal fields—even the staid *American Law Review* gave twenty-eight pages to the trial in the January, 1877, issue—and the people of Pennsylvania showed their appreciation in letters, speeches and demonstrations. As for McParland, he had the satisfaction of having done an extremely difficult task and done it well, although he was to suffer physically for the rest of his life, as a result of his work in the coal fields.

A grateful employer, Pinkerton sent McParland to Denver hoping that the clear mountain air would help him regain his health. As previously mentioned, McParland eventually became head of the Agency's branch in that city, specializing in the ways of outlaws. Still fearing that his operative might be the target of a vengeful bullet fired by one of the disbanded brotherhood, Pinkerton hired as his bodyguard Charles Siringo, the famous cowboy detective and one of the deadliest shots in the West.

17

"We live in deeds, not years."
—Bailey

ALTHOUGH FAR FROM WELL, Allan Pinkerton still acted as general superintendent of the firm that he had founded, deploying operatives from the various branches of the Agency to battle criminals on both sides of the Atlantic. Now internationally famous, Pinkerton's National Detective Agency worked with England's Scotland Yard, the French Sureté and the police forces of other nations, besides co-operating with state and local law-enforcement authorities in the United States. However, Allan no longer automatically sent a dozen or more men to conduct an investigation. McParland's single-handed operation in the Mollie Maguire case had taught him that one man could successfully carry out an assignment. Of course, if a situation arose that demanded the services of a large number of operatives, Pinkerton employed them.

Actually, Allan resented sending operatives out on assignments while he remained at his desk. He much pre-

ferred working in the field, too. Therefore, despite warnings from his doctor, he would occasionally undertake to
trail a lawbreaker himself, but for the most part he devoted himself to supervisory activities. There was plenty
for him to do. Not only had the Agency's activities expanded to include overseas operations, but hundreds of
new clients had to be served as well, while local police
departments—as they had done for years—were constantly
asking for help. Moreover, from time to time, the United
States Government asked the former head of the secret
service to undertake a special mission.

One of these assignments followed the election of 1880.
In that year, the Republican candidate, James A. Garfield,
a former schoolteacher, defeated Winfield S. Hancock,
who, like his opponent, had built up an outstanding record in the War Between the States. The campaign had
been marked by political deals and an assessment on all
federal officeholders of five per cent of their annual sal-
aries. The politicians made it clear to Federal employees
that they owed their jobs to a political party and, therefore, they should contribute to that party's campaign fund.
This practice completely ignored the civil service reforms
instituted by President Rutherford B. Hayes in 1877. At
that time, Hayes issued an executive order forbidding any
political activity on the part of the government workers
except voting and expressing their opinions.

After assuming office, Garfield paid little attention to
the civil service reforms instituted by his predecessor. He
did, however, sponsor an investigation of frauds in the
Post Office Department and asked the Pinkerton organization to check contracts signed by federal officials covering the "star routes." These were the rural mail routes
in the South and West where there were no railroads and
postal material had to be carried by stage. Sometimes,

shortly after a contract was signed, the amount of mail to
a certain locality would increase substantially—as in the
case of a small town that suddenly became the center of
a gold rush—and the carrier would lose money. In order
to be fair to the contractors, the Congress had passed leg-
islation that, if such a situation arose, the Postmaster
General could increase payments for service on "star
routes" without awarding new contracts.

Technically, this was an admirable arrangement, but,
actually, it led to corruption. Dishonest contractors would
deliberately bid ridiculously low figures for certain routes,
be awarded them, service them for a short period and
then ask the Second Assistant Postmaster General for an
adjustment. Such increases were always granted, but
rarely were they justified. Usually, they were far in excess
of equitable adjustment. On one group of contracts covering 134 routes, the government was defrauded out of
nearly five million dollars. This tremendous sum was split
between the contractors and their confederates in the Post
Office Department.

Under Pinkerton's direction, Agency operatives discovered that, although one western "star route" only brought
in $761 in a year, the contractor who served it received
$50,000 for his work! While this was bad enough, the in-
vestigators learned that, for thirty-nine days, not a single
letter was transported over this particular route. Another
contractor's figures did not seem to bother anyone in the
Post Office Department, but they seemed quite fantastic
to honest Allan Pinkerton. They showed that each of
the contractor's horses worked twenty hours a day and
that their driver worked forty hours daily.

"The Pinks," following Allan's directions, secured a mass
of evidence that showed the existence of an agreement between men in high positions in the government and the

contractors to raise payments for delivering mail on the "star routes" and to divide the extra profits among themselves. As a result, President Garfield's Postmaster General, Thomas L. James, who had made a reputation as the "reform postmaster" of New York City, took the conspirators to court and twenty-five of the swindlers were indicted. Because of political pressure, their trials dragged through one hearing after another and only one of all those accused was convicted of fraud against the government. However, Pinkerton's investigation helped pave the way for widespread reform of the civil service and drew the public's attention to the need of having men of integrity in positions of trust.

While working on the "star route" frauds, Pinkerton also managed to find time to direct investigations dealing with thefts from express companies and false insurance claims. As always, he noticed clues that others had missed and his vivid imagination suggested ways to make suspects confess. Somehow, Allan always knew that, although a lock was broken, a door forced or a messenger carrying vast sums of money chloroformed, they were false clues and the crime was an "inside job." The master sleuth also knew when to give a culprit a friendly talk or to handcuff him to an operative—who had orders not to speak to his prisoner—until the constant silence broke down the criminal and he confessed.

Busy when he should have been resting, Pinkerton continued to hound criminals of all types. Then, one morning in May, 1884, Allan, as usual, left his home at 554 West Munroe Street, in Chicago, to take his customary morning walk. In some unexplained fashion, he tripped, bit his tongue, and gangrene developed. After three weeks of intense suffering, Allan Pinkerton, founder of the oldest private detective agency in the world, died on July 1, 1884. He was buried in Graceland Cemetery, Chicago.

When his will was read, it was disclosed that the immigrant cooper, who had come to the United States with only a single dollar, had left an estate of half a million. Yet, this was but a fraction of the fortune Allan Pinkerton might have accumulated over the years. His honesty had prevented him from taking bribes, as so many law-enforcement officers did in the period from the War Between the States to the outbreak of World War I. Moreover, his sense of fairness had not permitted him to accept rewards for capturing criminals clients had hired him to apprehend.

Most of Pinkerton's money went to his wife, who survived him by two years. His sons, as previously arranged, inherited the Agency. Joan Pinkerton had little need for her father's estate. She had married William Chalmers, an extremely wealthy Chicagoan. The former belle of Chicago's West Side and her husband were drawn together by their mutual love of music. Joan had acquired hers from her mother, who had been a choir and concert singer in both Edinburgh and Glasgow before leaving Scotland. Together, the Chalmers played an important part in organizing the Chicago Opera Company, which was, at one time, among the most outstanding operatic groups in the United States.

Unlike her father and brothers, Joan Pinkerton Chalmers did not make friends easily. Although she was well-known in Chicago social circles, few dared to call her by her first name. In fact, her only close friend was Mary Garden, the internationally famous Scottish-born American operatic soprano, who, in addition to being "a dramatic singer of power and distinction, excelling in spontaneity, artistic detail and striking delineation," served for a time as general director of the Chicago opera association. As a young girl, Joan had been known as "the queen of the West Side" and, as Mrs. Chalmers, she acted like one. She ruled her family with an iron hand and, when angered, her deep blue eyes, under their black brows, would flash with almost the same brilliance as did the diamonds in the tiara she wore while attending the opera. Yet, on occasion, Pinkerton's autocratic, high-tempered daughter could unbend—at the age of eighty she danced a cakewalk!

Along with the Agency, William and Robert Pinkerton had another legacy from their father. This was their personal intense hatred for criminals. They also inherited from Allan a sense of duty that drove them to personally take the responsibility of tracking down and capturing dangerous desperadoes, rather than assigning such missions to their employees. Therefore, upon assuming control of Pinkerton's National Detective Agency, following the death of the firm's founder, they not only directed its ever-expanding scope of activities in the eighteen-eighties, eighteen-nineties and early nineteen hundreds, but also spent much time in the field.

There was absolutely no friction between William and Robert. They worked together as co-owners of the Agency with the same co-operation that they had shown when, as young men of twenty-two and twenty, respectively, they had ingeniously solved their first case—the Tennessee train robbery. Robert, who had frequently undertaken daring assignments in the Pennsylvania coal fields during McParland's brave investigation of the Mollie Maguires, operated out of the Chicago office. However, he often represented the Agency abroad and traveled all over Europe and the Near East, seeking criminals who had fled America. Many of these wanted men, knowing

that Bob Pinkerton had crossed half a continent and the
Atlantic Ocean to trail them, surrendered voluntarily
rather than fight extradition. They realized that, sooner
or later, the younger Pinkerton brother would find some
way of causing them to be deported to the United States
as undesirable persons.

Actually, this respect and fear of the dogged determination and detecting ability of "The Pinks" was nothing
new. From the earliest days of the Agency, petty thieves
and master criminals alike had been afraid of the men
who proudly wore the Pinkerton badge. Writing in 1895,
George White, one of the most notorious safe-crackers of
all times, summed up the attitude of lawbreakers toward
the Pinkertons in his memoirs:

> In those days (1869-70) this private detective agency was
> as yet in its infancy in New York but had attracted a great
> deal of attention from the public for its honesty. Strictly
> speaking, I hated the Pinkertons as thoroughly as the cor-
> rupt police did because of their interference with my pro-
> fessional duties. Many a time I had been enraged and
> beaten out of thousands by the popping up of one or more
> of the Agency's men.
> Nevertheless, I had to acknowledge that they were hon-
> est and it was dangerous for a crook when a Pinkerton was
> on his trail.

The chances are that the senior Pinkerton read this
praise of his organization by a convicted robber in *From
Boniface to Bank Robber,* the story of White's career
from his ownership of the Central House, in Stoneham,
Massachusetts, to his release from the penitentiary, because "Whitey the Wise" was of particular interest to Allan. Not only did this master criminal advise others how
to "crack a jug," he also assisted his friends in escaping
from prison. Once, after arranging for a former confed-

William Pinkerton subdues a band of robbers although shot in the side.

erate to be smuggled past guards and through gates in an empty barrel, White boldly accompanied him to New York City. There was little danger of the climax to his unusual plan failing. White handcuffed his friend and provided himself with forged credentials that identified him as a member of the secret service. The pair traveled in style to their destination, all the way from Columbus, Ohio!

Allan had another reason for reading White's book. The author had been associated with Shinburn in the Ocean National Bank robbery. Nevertheless, the compliments that "Whitey the Wise" paid the Pinkertons probably delighted the chief detective. Moreover, if anyone asked him why criminals such as White had so much respect for the Agency, he most likely would have replied that his firm was "ultimately successful in maintaining the dignity of the law" because of his operatives' "well-directed and untiring energy" and their policy "not to yield until success was assured."

No member of "The Pinks" had more energy and stubbornness when investigating a crime than did Allan Pinkerton's sons. Between Robert in the Chicago office and William in the New York City branch, clients were well served. Trained by their father from the time they were teen-agers, they had, in the years just previous to his death, worked with him on some of the most complicated cases in the history of the Agency.

While both brothers were outstanding detectives, William was, in some ways, a better sleuth than Robert. In fact, many students of the history of the development of modern police procedures consider William the most capable of the three original Pinkertons. As he grew older, Billy relied on his vast knowledge of criminals and their methods of operation and the importance of physical clues, but in his youth, he much preferred the excitement and adventure of hunting them down in person. Brave, daring and strong, he narrowly escaped death many times in hand-to-hand fights with outlaws armed with knives or in gun duels.

William needed all his boldness in 1870, when, with Pat O'Connell, a famous express company detective, he ploughed through the swamps along the Mississippi River. The two were seeking Hilary Farrington, who, with his brother Levi, had held up a Mobile and Ohio train and had taken $20,000 from the express car. Finally, the two sleuths caught up with their quarry in a farmhouse. After a long siege, they captured him. Handcuffed, the bandit was taken aboard a stern-wheeler, but he broke loose and grappled with William. Detective and outlaw battled fiercely all over the deck until Farrington, trying to club Pinkerton with the butt of a gun, lost his balance, tumbled over the rail and fell into the paddles of the river boat.

Although naturally a man of action, William could be infinitely patient. He worked on one case for twenty-five years, first with his father and then alone, concluding it seventeen years after Allan Pinkerton's death. No other case in the history of the Agency took as long to conclude as this one or provided the Pinkertons with better arguments for the need of international extradition treaties. Nor were Allan and his sons ever pitted against a more formidable adversary.

The individual who for a quarter of a century thwarted every attempt of the Pinkertons to take him into custody was Adam Worth. Nicknamed "Little Adam," Worth was considered by his associates and law-enforcement officers all over the globe as "the emperor of the underworld." He deserved the title. While estimates vary as to the amount of money Worth stole or realized by forgeries and swindles during his long criminal career—the range from $4,-000,000 to $8,000,000—all historians of crime agree that he never spent a single day in jail.

Worth was a hard-working clerk until the outbreak of the War Between the States. He was no patriot and had no desire to answer Lincoln's call for volunteers. Nevertheless, he willingly enlisted, joining the ranks of the "bounty jumpers." This was the term applied to unprincipled men who would enlist in the Union Army, receive several hundred dollars as a bonus for volunteering, then immediately desert. A few days later, they would re-enlist under assumed names, in order to collect another bounty. The ease with which he hoodwinked the recruiting officers convinced Worth that crime paid, and paid well—he got $500 the second time he joined the army—so, after his final discharge, he never did an honest day's work.

In the years following the meeting of Grant and Lee under the apple tree at Appomattox Court House and the surrender of the Confederacy, Worth was the leader of a band of bank robbers that carried out spectacular raids on "burglar-proof" vaults all over the country. However, Pinkerton's National Detective Agency had nothing about "Little Adam" in its files until after he directed the robbery of the Boylston Bank, in Boston, Massachusetts. During their investigation of this crime, the Pinkertons apprehended some of Worth's accomplices, who, hoping to receive light sentences, told the detectives all about their leader. He had, they informed their captors, taken his share of the money belonging to the depositors of the Boston bank—slightly over $100,000—and his loot from other robberies and fled to England, where he planned to live like a wealthy gentleman.

Pinkerton operatives were on the next boat sailing from New York City for London. In the British capital they

had no difficulty locating Worth. Discreet inquiries revealed that "Little Adam" had no intention of ever returning to the United States. He had abdicated his throne as
"the emperor of the underworld." Worth made it plain
that he had only one desire—to live quietly, never pick another lock, blast another safe or sell another forged bond.

There was no doubt in the detectives' minds that, with
Worth's vast illicit fortune and the lack of an extradition
treaty between the United Kingdom and the United
States, he could achieve his ambition. He had, in addition to plenty of money, all the necessary qualifications to
pass as a cultivated gentleman. He was personable, well-
mannered and charming.

However, neither the Pinkertons nor Worth realized
that "Little Adam" was to be blackmailed by former confederates for the rest of his life. They were to badger him
constantly, demanding money in person, and in letters
written from prison cells. Fearful that, if he did not ac-
cede to his ex-collaborators' requests, they would disclose
his true identity, Worth met every demand upon his pock-
etbook. At last, in order to escape the continual claims
upon his "loyalty" and cash reserves, "Little Adam" tried
to disappear. He bought a yacht and spent as much time
as possible at sea. But whenever he put into a port for
supplies, a partner in an almost forgotten crime would
be waiting on the dock and greet him with a request for
money.

Consequently, despite the fact that he had brought
nearly half a million dollars with him to England, Worth's
bank account dwindled rapidly as he bought the silence
of his one-time associates. In order to recoup his fortune,
"Little Adam" was forced to forget his retirement plans
and resume his criminal activities.

It only took two fresh daring robberies to make up his

losses, however. In the first, he abstracted $400,000 worth of uncut stones from the Kimberley "diamond mail" in South Africa. Then, shortly afterwards, he robbed a London post office of another valuable shipment of diamonds. In order to dispose of his illegal accumulation of precious gems, Worth, using another criminal as a "front," went into the jewelry business. Frequently his accomplice sold diamond merchants the very stones that they had expected to receive in the mails which Worth had robbed! After a year and a half "Little Adam" no longer had any of the stolen stones in his possession. However, in their place he had a tremendous sum of money and a greater fear than ever that his past would be revealed.

His fears were justified. Chapman, Becker and Elliott, three former partners in crime, arrested in Turkey, sent word by the speedy underworld telegraph that, unless Worth came to their aid, Scotland Yard would take him into custody on "information received." Worth had no more desire to become an inmate of a British prison than he had to enter an American one. Therefore, he provided his friends with enough money to bribe their way to freedom, hoping that he would never hear from them again. To his consternation, upon leaving Turkey, Chapman, Becker and Elliott came to London, resumed their criminal careers and were arrested once more. The doors of their cells were barely shut when the trio again asked "Little Adam" for help.

Worth realized that it would be impossible to bribe English authorities, but he also knew that, if he didn't rescue his friends, he too would soon be wearing prison garb, instead of well-tailored suits. Frantic, he sought desperately for some way out of the situation. Finally, he plotted—and soon carried out—one of the most unique crimes in history.

On a foggy May night in 1876, just as the two hands of the clock in the tower of the Houses of Parliament pointed straight up and Big Ben tolled the hour of twelve, Adam Worth furtively hurried down Bond Street. A few minutes later, he was crawling up the side of the building that housed the internationally famous art gallery of Messrs. Agnew and Company. Sure-footed as a cat, Worth made his way to the second story, forced open a window and entered the gallery. Carefully shielding his lantern so that its glow could not be seen by a passing policeman if the fog lifted, "Little Adam" cut Gainsborough's portrait of the Duchess of Devonshire from its frame, painstakingly rolled the canvas up and placed it in a metal tube.

Worth's original intention had been to arrange a compromise with the Home Secretary of England. He would return the picture if Chapman, Becker and Elliott were released and there was no prosecution for the theft of the portrait. The second condition presented no difficulties. The owners of the gallery, who valued the Gainsborough masterpiece at $50,000—it is worth far more today—offered a reward of $5,000 for its return and promised to ask no questions. The Messrs. Agnew made it perfectly clear that they were not the least bit interested in having the thief arrested, all they wanted was to regain possession of the portrait. "Little Adam" had a question to pose, even if the art dealers had no desire to pry. Worth wanted to know whether Chapman, Becker and Elliott would be released if the Duchess of Devonshire's portrait was restored to its rightful owners. Scotland Yard had the answer. It was "No!"

Because Worth was an American and his criminal record in the United States was now common knowledge, the proprietors of the gallery engaged Pinkerton's National Detective Agency in hopes of regaining the painting. Allan, William and Robert, along with a dozen operatives, tried vainly to get possession of the "Duchess of Devonshire," as did crack agents of the Criminal Investigation Department at Scotland Yard, the headquarters of Britain's law-enforcement force. Yet, although hounded by both English detectives and "The Pinks," Worth was not too concerned with his possible arrest. In fact, he felt safer than at any other time during his forty-odd years as a criminal. "Little Adam" found that he had stolen an insurance policy. "If I am taken into custody," he warned the authorities, "the Gainsborough picture will be destroyed."

For twenty-five years the stalemate continued. Then, in 1901, Pat Sheedy, gambler and one-time close friend of Worth, called at the Agency's Chicago office and asked to see William Pinkerton, with whom he was on familiar terms. Sheedy informed Billy that Worth and the "Duchess of Devonshire" were in a downtown hotel and he was positive "some arrangement could be made."

Disregarding his father's rule about compromising with a criminal—Allan had been dead for seventeen years— William arranged matters with Worth. Sheedy acted as the go-between. Finally, the metal tube containing Gainsborough's picture was exchanged for a wad of crisp new bank notes. How much Worth received was never made public.

Always reticent, William Pinkerton was particularly uncommunicative about his deal with Worth. The only person to whom he disclosed how much had been paid to ransom the "Duchess" was his brother, Robert. Nevertheless, no matter how high the figure was, there is no doubt that Moreland Agnew thought William had made an excellent bargain, for when, in answer to a cablegram, he crossed the Atlantic and half the American continent and nervously removed the portrait from its metallic container in William's office, it was in perfect condition.

* * *

While William ended the Agency's interest in "the emperor of the underworld" by negotiations, Robert paid no attention to protocol in his dealings with Walter Sheridan, heir apparent to Worth's throne. And he took care of this master thief himself. The younger Pinkerton waited until Sheridan disembarked one day from a Pennsylvania Railroad ferryboat, at the Desbrosses Street docks in New York City. Grasping the criminal's shoulder, he said quietly, "Sheridan, I want you to come with me to the Church Street police station. I have a bench warrant for your arrest."

Sheridan went quietly, but it was not until he was in a Sing Sing cell that the Pinkertons were content and positive that they would have no more trouble with him. At the time of his arrest, there were eighty-two indictments against Sheridan in the State of New York alone. No wonder Allan Pinkerton called this master criminal "an adept in the art of living genteelly from forced public contributions of a varied character."

Like Worth, Sheridan began his criminal career with a relatively minor offense. He stole a horse in St. Louis in 1858, was convicted, broke jail and escaped to Chicago. Here, he became a hotel thief, was arrested and served three years in the penitentiary at Alton. Upon his release, Sheridan, who was quite distinguished-looking, became the "stall" of a gang of bank robbers. His job was to distract the cashier's attention by asking a series of complicated questions about buying and selling bonds while his confederates sneaked in the bank vault and looted it. Another of his tricks was to stand behind someone making out a slip for a large cash deposit, tap him on the shoulder and politely call attention to the fact that a ten-dollar bill—thrown down by Sheridan—was on the floor. When the victim bent over to pick up the bank note, Sheridan would grab his money and rush out of the bank. There was little chance of Sheridan being caught. As he fled with the loot, the rest of the gang effectively blocked pursuit by "accidentally" getting in the way.

In Springfield, Illinois, the gang stole $32,000 and would have escaped with their booty, if one of their number, Charles Hicks, had not failed to cover the money completely with his overcoat. The roll of bills was spotted by a bank official and both Hicks and Sheridan were arrested. Sheridan jumped bail and the Pinkertons were called in to trace him. It was no easy task. All that the detectives had to go by were varying descriptions of the thief, and there was no picture of Sheridan in the Agency files.

Pinkerton, senior, suggested that Hicks' brother might provide a clue to Sheridan's whereabouts and the man was placed under surveillance. He was followed to Hudson, Michigan, where he went to a hotel which operatives learned was owned by Sheridan and managed by his brother-in-law. That night, "A small and, under the circumstances, quite excusable burglary" took place. A picture of Sheridan was taken off the wall of the manager's office and placed in the Agency's files.

Eventually, Sheridan was arrested in Sandusky, Ohio. After being handcuffed and taken aboard a Chicago-bound train, he almost convinced the other passengers that he was being kidnaped. He then offered his guard $10,000 in cash to let him jump through the train window. The offer was refused. Although both attempts to escape from the Pinkertons had failed, Sheridan had no intention of standing trial for bank robbery.

In Chicago, William Pinkerton took the prisoner into his father's private office and then left him, knowing that he could not get away. Sheridan seized the snuffbox on Allan's desk, planning to throw its contents into Billy's eyes when he returned. His scheme failed, for William came into the room with his revolver drawn. Sheridan nonchalantly took a pinch of snuff, then replaced the box on the desk and politely remarked, "Billy, this snuff of your father's is excellent stuff."

"For the eyes?" William asked.

"Eyes or nose," was the quick reply. "But I'm very sorry to say that the *noes* have it this time!"

Brought to trial, Sheridan, by legal maneuvering and widespread bribery, secured a verdict of not guilty. He celebrated by assembling a gang of bank robbers. In a few months, Sheridan's share of their loot was over a quarter of a million dollars. His next illegal business venture was the organization of the most gigantic forgery in the history of American crime, the counterfeiting of bonds issued by leading corporations in the United States. These forgeries were masterpieces of the engraver's art and were so perfectly executed that many of them were even bought by officers in the companies on which they were drawn.

The gang disposed of nearly half of the five million dollars' worth of bogus securities they had manufactured. With his profits, Sheridan bought a seat on the New York Produce Exchange and he also became an importer of Belgian marble. However, in time, the worthlessness of the bonds was discovered and he fled to Belgium, which had no extradition treaty with the United States and was, therefore, in Allan Pinkerton's words, a "fashionable retreat for Americans having too little honesty and too much brains."

Under the name of Walter Stewart, Sheridan eventually returned to this country and established a huge hothouse in Denver, Colorado, raising vegetables and rare plants for market. Before long, he owned a bank and was a very successful and highly regarded businessman, but reckless speculation in mining stocks ruined him. "The Pinks," who had been looking for Sheridan ever since he left Belgium, caught up with him when he left Denver and came east to recruit a new gang of "bank bursters," in hopes of accumulating another fortune.

He might have succeeded—but Robert Pinkerton was waiting at the ferryboat!

* * *

William and Robert also played an important part in apprehending the Bidwells, who defrauded the Bank of England of a huge sum of money by means of a complicated series of forgeries. Incidentally, Sheridan had originally plotted this swindle, but withdrew because he did not trust the Bidwells. Perhaps George and Austin Bidwell were not trustworthy, but they led the Agency into its most extensive operation before they were placed in the prisoners' dock.

Pinkerton's National Detective Agency was retained by the "Old Lady of Threadneedle Street"—the affectionate nickname Englishmen have given to the Bank of England —to find the Bidwells, in case they were in America. Even Allan, in the early days of the Agency, would have approved of the campaign that followed. Robert and a select party of assistants co-operated with the men of Scotland Yard in London, while William directed a widespread search throughout the United States and the West Indies. By painstaking checking and rechecking of passenger lists, comparing the handwriting on the forgeries with the contents of wastepaper baskets and engaging in a dispute with Spanish officials in Cuba, the Pinkertons finally located Austin Bidwell. His brother was arrested in Ireland.

Tried and convicted, the Bidwells were given life imprisonment. Later, their sentence was reduced as being excessively harsh. Among those who worked for their release was John Bright, the famous English orator, reformer and statesman who, by his speeches in the House of Commons, greatly helped the Northern cause during the War Between the States.

* * *

The work of the Pinkerton Agency in the Bank of England forgeries case added greatly to its reputation overseas. Meanwhile, at home, the firm would have had, in all probability, a far greater number of bank robberies, swindles and other crimes to investigate if it had not been for the personal respect that William Pinkerton commanded. Everyone who knew Billy—his friends and acquaintances ranged from police chiefs to underworld figures—realized that, although William was not talkative, he meant everything he did say. Therefore, criminals listened when Billy let it be known that criminals had nothing to fear from the Agency, providing they stayed away from its clients, but if anyone stole a cent from a firm that engaged the Pinkertons, he would be trailed, arrested and taken into court.

Like his father, Billy had a phenomenal memory for faces and could recognize a petty rogue or an international crook when seeing him for the first time, if he had ever come across his picture in the Agency's files. William also had a remarkable knowledge of the ways of the underworld and the various techniques of its residents. When Anna Held, the famous actress, reported that her collection of jewels valued at $200,000 had been stolen, all Billy Pinkerton did was make a telephone call. The next day, the jewels were returned.

However, as the years passed, Pinkerton's National Detective Agency did less and less chasing of criminals, although it continued to play an important part in the capture and conviction of some of the most notorious lawbreakers in the annals of crime. The shift in the Agency's major activities was made for two reasons. Because of the development of well-organized and carefully trained law-enforcement bodies throughout the country, it was no longer necessary for local authorities to call in the Pinkerton detectives when a major crime was committed. Moreover, the Pinkerton brothers deliberately set out to expand a service to business firms, industrial plants and large corporations which had been inaugurated by their father. In return for a yearly retainer, the Agency promised a client protection and, if necessary, the immediate investigation of any crime committed against its property. In order to provide efficient service to those subscribing to this arrangement, William and Robert opened several branch offices in various parts of the country.

Unfortunately, providing security for factories and corporations sometimes involved the Pinkertons in the conflict between labor and management during the years when trade unionism was making its first demands for better working conditions, higher pay and shorter working hours. Luckily, while protecting the interests of management, Pinkerton's National Detective Agency avoided serious trouble during strikes and riots until 1892. In that year, the founder's sons accepted an assignment from a large corporation and, in two days, almost completely ruined the reputation of the Agency that Allan Pinkerton had so zealously guarded!

18

WE NEVER SLEEP

*"Meddling with another man's folly
is always thankless work."*
—Kipling

IT IS EXTREMELY DOUBTFUL that, had Allan Pinkerton
been alive in the spring of 1892, he would have accepted the commission Henry C. Frick, chairman of
Carnegie Brothers & Company and a bitter enemy of organized labor, offered his sons. A canny Scot, Allan would
have realized this was one assignment that would bring
no profit and much abuse to the Agency.

Not since May, 1886, when the Haymarket affair rocked
the city of Chicago and shocked and terrified the entire
nation, was there so much ill-feeling between workingmen
and their employers. The steelworkers—skilled men and
union members alike—were engaged in a bitter struggle
with the Carnegie Company over wages and union recognition. Feeling on both sides was high. While negotiating
with representatives of his employees, Frick contacted
Robert Pinkerton and inquired if it were possible to hire

three hundred men to protect the Carnegie plant at Homestead, Pennsylvania, a town eight miles east of Pittsburgh.

Homestead was an outstanding example of American industrial technology. The plant used iron and coal from its own mines, transporting them to the plant, either by a fleet of company-owned Great Lakes steamers or by a private railroad line four hundred and twenty-five miles long. Here the ore was smelted with coke made in Homestead ovens and with limestone from Homestead-operated quarries.

After weeks of meetings, negotiations between the employees and the company broke down. The more rowdy elements among the workers paraded through the streets of Homestead and hung Frick in effigy. As a punishment, the company shut the plant down, though the men were still working under their old wage contract. The shutting down of plants was a common weapon of employers in former years and was known as a "lockout," which is best defined as the refusal of an employer to allow his help to come to work unless there is an agreement on terms.

There is no doubt that Frick's action would have been repugnant to Allan Pinkerton's sense of fair play. Moreover, despite the fact that the master sleuth had acquired both fame and fortune by working for some of the nation's leading corporations, he had never forgotten his activities as a radical Chartist in his youth. "I know," he once wrote, "what it is from personal experience, to be a tramp journeyman; to carry the stick and the bundle; to seek work and not get it; and to get it, and receive but a pittance for it, or suddenly lose it altogether and be compelled to resume the weary search. In fact, I know every bitter experience that the most laborious of laboring men have been or ever will be required to undergo. . . ."

However, Allan had been dead for eight years when the Pinkerton Agency signed a contract with the Carnegie Company promising to send three hundred men to the Homestead works. While a handful of trained operatives would be included, the majority of the guards would be temporary employees, hired for five dollars a day. There was no difficulty recruiting the men, but it might have been different if they had known that, after the company erected a high board fence around the plant, the locked-out workers would knock holes in it as high as a man's shoulder and big enough to admit the barrel of a rifle!

The Agency was to send the "five-dollars-a-day Pinkertons" to Ashtabula, Ohio, where a special train would carry them to Youngstown. Here, they would board company boats and steam to Homestead by way of the Mahoning and Monongahela Rivers. The ships were due to dock on the sixth of July. Sheriff McLeary was prepared for their coming through a formal request from the company that the three hundred guards be deputized. Unawed by the demands of Big Business and not expecting any violence, the sheriff refused, but pledged that he would have the plant guarded by his own men.

McLeary and his deputies made an inspection tour around the plant. They found nothing amiss. The steelworkers, on strike since July first, were merely picketing the works, they reported. Union leaders offered the sheriff every co-operation. They would, if he were willing, serve as deputies and post a bond to insure that they would carry out their duties in a proper manner. The offer was refused, McLeary making it plain that he wanted no more deputies and that he was very much against the importation of outside guards by the company.

There is little doubt that the sheriff sincerely believed that there was no danger of violence breaking out and that, if it did, he would be able to handle the situation. Moreover, he felt that, sooner or later, strikers and Carnegie Company officials would compromise and the plant would be reopened.

Whether it would or not, no one knows. On two barges, normally used by the company to ship railroad rails from the mills at Braddock—site of the defeat of General Braddock by the French and Indians in colonial days—a cargo of terror was being transported to Homestead. The barges had been converted into miniature naval vessels. Their holds were filled with bunks, and galleys had been set up. The hulls had been lined with the heaviest steel plate the Carnegie Company manufactured and stocked with an arsenal of hundreds of rifles and revolvers. Early in the morning of July 6, towed by the steam tugs *Tide* and *Little Bill,* the barges approached the wharf at Homestead.

The strikers, in true naval tradition, had sent out a patrol boat. Its lookout spotted the *Little Bill* dragging both barges—the other tug's engine having failed near Pittsburgh—and gave the alarm by sounding a steam whistle. Before the shrill screech died away, every bell and whistle in town echoed its warning. Long before the *Little Bill* neared shore, the river banks were lined with the residents of Homestead.

Suddenly, a shot rang out. To this day, despite careful investigations by the Pinkertons and the Congress of the United States, no one knows whether it came from one of the barges or from the shore. At any rate, it marked the beginning of one of the most unhappy incidents in the economic history of the country.

When the smoke cleared, there were dead and wounded on both barges and banks. During a lull in the battle, the *Little Bill* collected the Pinkerton wounded, turned about and, with throttle wide open, returned to Braddock.

Meanwhile, both sides regrouped their forces and resumed firing. An assault party of Pinkertons attempted to storm ashore, but was driven off with heavy losses by sharp-shooting strikers concealed behind hastily erected barricades.

The sniping continued for several hours, then the heavy artillery was brought into action. From some source, the steelworkers had secured a small brass cannon which subjected the *Little Bill* to such a heavy barrage when it returned in hopes of drawing the two barges back to Braddock, that the attempt was abandoned. Unable to steer because of the shot and shell whizzing through the pilothouse, the captain threw himself down on the deck and let his vessel drift downstream until it was out of range.

However, the barges offered easy targets and they were raked with bullets. Furious because they felt that the company had hired a "private army" to end the strike under the guise of having it guard the plant and caught in the grip of excitement, the steelworkers were determined to slaughter every man on board. One group of strikers poured hundreds of barrels of oil on the river, set it afire and waited for the flames to destroy the barges. Their scheme failed because a breeze came up and blew the inferno in the opposite direction. Another party of workers tried to lay a natural gas line toward the barges, planning to saturate them with gas, then explode it, but they were held off by rifle fire.

The thud of bullets and the boom of the cannon died down about noon—for even soldiers must eat. While the strikers munched food brought by their womenfolk, the men on the barges raised a white flag. It was too good a target to resist. Sandwiches were set aside and sticks of dynamite flung at the appeal for a truce. Then, after finishing their lunches, the snipers picked up their rifles.

By mid-afternoon, only spasmodic firing could be heard in Homestead. The strikers heard instead long, loud and levelheaded speeches from the heads of their union. According to their leaders, the fighters were not helping the cause of the workingman in general nor that of the Amalgamated Association of Iron and Steel Workers in particular. The battle must stop and the wounded men on the barges be given medical attention. Most of the strikers paid no attention to their elected leaders, but continued to man their barricades. Finally, Hugh O'Donnell, a Homestead man and an officer of the union, gave a fiery oration, holding an American flag in one hand, while he pounded his points home with the other. When he stopped talking, the strikers agreed to let the Pinkerton group surrender.

O'Donnell arranged that the men on the barges could come ashore with all their personal property, but insisted that all guns and ammunition remain on board. No sooner had the two hundred and thirty-four Pinkerton employees disembarked, than the mob swarmed over the barges, seized everything movable, then set the boats afire. As O'Donnell led the Pinkertons to the local skating rink, where he planned to have the wounded cared for until transportation out of Homestead could be arranged, they suffered further casualties. As the men filed down the street, they were assaulted with weapons of all kinds, wielded by women as well as men. As a result, although only twenty-one Pinkertons had been hit by bullets, when the doctors arrived at the skating-rink, they had one hundred and thirty-four patients to treat! Eighteen strikers had also been wounded. The dead totaled twenty—eleven steelworkers and nine Pinkertons.

Finally, O'Donnell, aided by other union leaders and the more levelheaded members of their group, brought peace to Homestead. At midnight, all the invaders were placed upon a Pittsburgh-bound train and the Pinkertons rode out of Homestead into a Congressional inquiry—and the hatred of organized labor until comparatively recent years.

When Robert and William appeared at the Congressional hearing into the Homestead affair on July 23rd, the elder brother acted as spokesman. He gave facts and figures up to a point, but never one to talk much, he refused to make public the details of the Agency's contract with the Carnegie Company. His father would have found this loyalty to a client the one thing worthy of approval in the entire incident. However, Allan would not have been pleased to read the political platform of the Populist Party in the campaign of 1892. Along with promising a reduction in the length of the working day, the Populists, with an eye on the growing labor vote, condemned the use of Pinkertons in labor disputes.

19

"The old order changeth, yielding place to new."
—Alfred, Lord Tennyson

B**Y** 1907—the year of Robert Pinkerton's death—the
Agency had overcome much of the unfavorable public reaction to its part in the Homestead riot. William, who
assumed management of the firm following his brother's
death, steadfastly refused to accept any security assignments that might be construed as strikebreaking, despite
the ever-increasing demands of clients for protection by
Pinkerton's Guard Service.

The Guard Service was one of the oldest branches of
the parent organization, having been formed by Allan
Pinkerton in 1850. He called it "Pinkerton's Protective Patrol" and contracted to furnish, for a daily fee, uniformed
guards to individuals and business concerns. While the
Guard Service never received the publicity given to Pinkerton operatives who outshot train robbers and outsmarted
swindlers, over the years it became a major source of reve-
nue to the Agency.

As he guided the organization back into public favor, William was aided by his nephew. Robert's son had a great deal to live up to, including his name, Allan Pinkerton. The young man soon proved that, like his father and grandfather, he was a capable detective and, after William's death in 1923, he became president of the Agency when it was reorganized as a corporation.

Like the original Allan Pinkerton, the first president of the Agency was a lover of horses and this led to his being commissioned by racing associations to investigate suspected misconduct on the part of owners, trainers and jockeys and to keep the tracks clear of pickpockets, touts and bookmakers. By degrees, the Agency established a department to handle this business. Today, its complex activities range from checking the character of race-track employees to helping veterinarians give saliva tests to horses, in order to determine whether they have been doped. In its attempt to make "The Sport of Kings" free from crime, the Racing Department maintains a typical Pinkerton file, where information about every active registered race horse is kept up-to-date.

One of the earliest of the undesirables that the second Allan Pinkerton barred from the tracks was Arnold Rothstein, the infamous gambler. Young Allan was to have further dealings with Rothstein when, in response to the request of President Johnson of the American League, the Agency investigated the so-called "Black Sox" scandal, following the World's Series in 1919. A true sportsman, Pinkerton could understand thoroughly the heartbroken appeal of the little boy who, having heard that his idol, "Shoeless Joe" Jackson, had accepted Rothstein's bribe to "throw" the series, tearfully pleaded, "Say it ain't so, Joe."

Just as the original Allan served his country in the War Between the States, so did his namesake serve the United

States during World War II. As a major in the Intelligence Corps, Pinkerton was active in France. Like his grandfather, he was no armchair soldier and, while gathering military information, he was overcome by poison gas, which eventually caused his death in 1930. At that time, his son, Robert A. Pinkerton II, the great-grandson of the cooper from Dundee, became head of the Agency.

* * *

If it were possible for the first Allan Pinkerton to see the headquarters of the firm that bears his name, at 100 Church Street, New York City, he would be amazed. It is in a modern glass-and-steel building and has wall-to-wall carpeting on the floor—a far cry from the original office in Chicago, with its scuffed floors, battered desks and poor lighting.

Allan would also be astounded at the number of employees now on the Agency's roster. When he began operations in 1850, there were nine people on his staff. Today, there are approximately 13,000 employees in the forty-five branch offices maintained in the United States and Canada.

While plain furnishings have given way to modern décor and a handful of trusted agents to a complex corporation, one thing about Pinkerton's National Detective Agency has not changed. The code set up by Allan Pinkerton when he founded what is now the world's oldest and largest investigative and security organization is still in force. The chances are that Allan would also be glad to learn that the firm's gross profits now total about $30,000,-000 annually.

Today, the corporation gets only twenty per cent of its business from its detecting activities—once it was eighty per cent. Nevertheless, despite the build-up of local police forces and the F.B.I., Pinkerton's Agency still tracks down criminals with the same steadfastness of purpose it held back in the days of Jesse James. Most of the firm's modern criminal investigative work is for corporations, lawyers, stores and hotels. While some of these clients have only recently signed contracts with the Agency, others have depended upon the Pinkerton organization to protect them from criminals for years. The Jewelers Security Alliance has retained "The Pinks" since its formation seventy-five years ago, and from this long association has come the world's most complete file on jewel thieves and dealers in stolen jewelry ever assembled.

Modern Pinkerton operatives are far more apt to "shoot" a picture than a gun. The Agency is frequently called upon to do non-criminal investigations for lawyers and insurance companies, and a clear photograph often means the end of a fraudulent claim. Pinkerton files are filled with cases in which quick settlements were obtained, thanks to an operative's skill with a camera, including the one in which a young woman "crippled" in an accident was photographed checking her crutches at the baggage room in New York's Grand Central Station after testifying in the guise of an invalid all day in court!

Besides using cameras, the Agency also employs electronic devices and is constantly testing new inventions that may have security applications in its research laboratory. If any of these prove valuable, they are used to supplement the manpower that protects the property, operations and work forces of industrial plants, banks, refineries, hospitals, universities and museums. Uniformed Pinkerton guards also furnish protective service at fairs, expositions, race tracks and sports events. More than one thousand Pinkertons are on duty at the Army-Navy football game each year, as ticket takers and ushers and to protect the spectators.

The uniformed guard service tries to keep undesirable things from happening, such as fire, theft, vandalism and damage to property. Individual jobs today often require the same wide range of talents that were needed in the early years of the Agency. The Pinkerton guard at a small hospital has often been pressed into service by the nurses because of his knowledge of first aid, while the guards at a waterfront installation operate a ship-to-shore radio. Speaking of ships, the Pinkerton Agency provides protection for Admiral Dewey's flagship, the cruiser *Olympia*, now moored in the Delaware River, at Philadelphia.

While uniformed guards furnish security to such varied establishments as banks and quarries, plain-clothes operatives investigate everything from theft to patent infringement. You can also hire a Pinkerton operative, complete with white tie and tails, to guard the gifts at a wedding.

Allan Commercial Service, a branch of the Agency, specializes in tracking down fraudulent or excessive claims against insurance and casualty companies. Recovering stolen property and arranging for the arrest of the thief is another service the Agency furnishes its clients. It also provides them with a wide variety of non-criminal investigations. It offers an inspection service for stores, hotels, railroads, airlines and similar businesses and will "shop" employees, observing their relations with the public and checking their honesty. This includes the investigation of applicants for a position or candidates for promotion.

In fact, there is little that Pinkerton's National Detective Agency cannot do for a client. Of course, still true to its founder's code, it will not break any of the fundamental rules formulated by Allan in 1850. Moreover, following a Congressional inquiry into labor-management relations in

1937, Robert A. Pinkerton barred the Agency from ever again accepting undercover work that would involve the investigation of a labor union.

The only American member of the *Lique Internationale des Societés de Surveillance,* a world-wide federation of security organizations with membership limited to one firm from each nation, Pinkerton's National Detective Agency is proud of its international reputation. Yet it is far prouder of the part it has played in the history of the United States. From the War Between the States to the present time, when Pinkerton guards protect plants manufacturing top-secret devices, the Agency has served the nation well in war and peace.

There is every evidence that it will continue to do so— the morning after Pearl Harbor, Robert A. Pinkerton announced that, for the duration of the war, the Agency would furnish its protective services to firms engaged in defense work at cost. Allan Pinkerton would have approved highly of his great-grandson's wish not to profit "from the deplorable world conditions or to demand high rates for our services because we know they must be accepted." After all, he too had given up private gain for the good of his country.

Index

Adams Express Company, 30-42, 130-132, 172

"Allen, E. J.," 70, 75, 77, 79, 91-93, 95-99, 103-106, 112, 114

Baltimore Plot, 50-64

Bangs, George H., 38, 44, 50-51, 60, 119, 132, 147, 150, 153, 155-156, 163-164

Beauregard, General Pierre, 77, 89

Benjamin, Judah P., 106

Bertillon, Alphonse, 140

Bonaparte, Napoleon, 144

Booth, John Wilkes, 117

Bright, John, 223

Brown, John, 32, 45-47

Buchanan, James, 57

Burnside, General Ambrose, 114, 115

Butler, General James, 84

Calhoun, John, 86, 87, 88

Cameron, Simon, 77, 103, 105

Carnegie Brothers & Company, 226

Chalmers, Joan Pinkerton, 4, 20, 208-209

Chalmers, William, 208

Chartist Movement, 3

Clay, Henry, 84

Compromise of 1850, 84

Dalton Gang, 181

Davis, Jefferson, 87, 89, 99, 102, 116

Doyle, Sir Arthur Conan, 186-187

"Duchess of Devonshire," 217

Felton, Samuel M., 49, 53, 61

Fort McHenry, 110

Fort Sumter, 65

Fugitive Slave Law, 17

Garden, Mary 208

Garfield, James A., 205

Grant, General Ulysses S., 114, 145

Greenhow, Rose, 86-102

Hale, Nathan, 68

Hamilton, Alexander, 22

239

SIGMUND A. LAVINE

was highly active while in college; he wrote features for the Boston *Sunday Post* and covered Boston University sports for two wire services. His parents were permanent members of John Craig's famous stock company, so, quite naturally, he played leads in Shakespeare productions and stage-managed five annual presentations of the Gilbert and Sullivan Association.

After receiving his M.A., he taught in a United States Government Indian School at Belcourt, North Dakota, for two years, learned to speak both the Sioux and Cree languages and talk in sign language. He was invited to tribal dances, ceremonies and Indian Court in reservations throughout Canada and the Northwest.

Sigmund Lavine has taught in the Boston Schools for over twenty years and is now an assistant principal. He also lectures and writes literary criticism.

With his wife, their teen-aged son Jerrold, Carrie, their whippet, and Andrea ben Ghazi, their prize-winning Afghan hound, he lives in a house filled with books, fish tanks and historical china. His family enjoys cruises to South America, cross-country motor trips and truck gardening on a piece of rocky New Hampshire land.